Tai Babilonia - 30th Anniversary

*NOTE - ZIG PINK CHIFFON
ON NUDE NET - CUTAWAY!

SILK CHIFFON SKIRT & SLEEVE

2002

Forever Two As One

Also by Martha Lowder Kimball:

Robin Cousins

With Toller Cranston:

Zero Tollerance

When Hell Freezes Over, Should I Bring My Skates?

Ice Cream: Thirty of the Most Interesting Skaters in History

Forever Two As One

Tai Babilonia & Randy Gardner
with Martha Lowder Kimball

MILLPOND
PRESS
2002

Text design and layout by Steve Meyer, Kristin Meyer and Martha Kimball

Please direct all correspondence and book orders to:
Millpond Press
258 McDaniel Ave.
Jamestown, NY 14701

Babilonia, Tai.
        Forever two as one / by Tai Babilonia, Randy Gardner with Martha Lowder Kimball
                p. cm.
Includes index.
        ISBN 0-9662502-1-4
    1. Babilonia, Tai. 2. Gardner, Randy, 1957-3. Skaters—United States—Bibliography.
I. Gardner, Randy, 1957-II. Kimball, Martha Lowder, 1946-III. Title.
        GV850.A2 B33 2002
        796.91'092'2—dc21
                                                        2002008944

Printed in Hong Kong

Dedications

To my family, Constancio Sr., Constancio Jr., and Cleo Babilonia, for rearranging your lives to accommodate my dreams of becoming a champion figure skater. You are my gold medal. I love you.

To Mabel Fairbanks. What you saw in Randy and me no one will really ever know. I feel your presence every day and know you are by my side always. Thank you for bribing Randy and me to hold each other's hand.

To Randy. There is so much more to us than what is in the poem—probably the most challenging, interesting, loving, and dysfunctional relationship I will ever be a part of. You were and always will be the wind beneath my wings. Here's to the next thirty years. Ha!

To Scout, my one and only. You have taught me so much about love, life, and myself. Everything got better and brighter when you arrived. You were my inspiration as I wrote this book. Now you will have something to share with your children. *Forever Two As One* is for you.

  —TRB

To Jan, Jack, and Gordy.

  —RG

To Mary Taylor Bush and her family for four decades of friendship and good times, and to the students of Jamestown High School who enriched my life.

  —MLK

Contents

Foreword

When I first contacted Tai and Randy in the summer of 1979, it was all really just beginning for them. They had recently won the world pairs skating title and were headed for the Olympics.

I always loved watching Tai and Randy skate. Part of me had wanted forever to be a classical dancer, and Tai skated just like a ballerina.

That summer I gave Tai a 24-karat-gold moon charm for good luck. She wore it on a chain around her neck and never took it off—not until just before Randy tried to skate injured at the 1980 Olympics in Lake Placid. I found that ironic. Randy was forced to withdraw from the competition, and of course Tai had to withdraw right along with him.

Besides sharing a love of ballet, Tai and I share longstanding relationships with our special working partners. The story of Tai's partnership with Randy is inspirational. It has inspired me to stay strong, to study ballet, and to learn to skate.

"We get a little bit better every day."

> Stevie Nicks
> Singer and songwriter

Acknowledgements

To Los Angeles. "There's no place like home."

To Mako Nakashima, my godfather, for introducing me to the frozen stage.

To Peggy Fleming, the first fairy princess I ever saw gliding across the ice. You inspired me to try again.

To the Gardner family. Everyone protects his or her baby cub differently. Now, as a parent myself, I completely understand. Thank you.

To Shelly McCladdie, Richard Ewell, Atoy Wilson, and Leslie Robinson. I watched and I learned.

To Al and Harriet De Ray, still very much a part of who I am today.

To the Los Angeles Figure Skating Club for believing in us.

To the USFSA for allowing us to compete and excel.

To the LAPD for the support and piggy banks.

To the Ice Capades Chalet, Santa Monica. Who could ask for a better place to train? If those walls could talk!

To Mr. Nicks. You made such an impression on me at an early age and still do today. You were intimidating, funny, caring, strict, classy, usually quiet, sometimes very loud, but, most of all, encouraging—the perfect ingredients to take Randy and me to the top. I love you!

To JoJo Starbuck and Ken Shelley. "Now, that's pairs skating." My absolute favorite pairs team, thank you for your love and support and, best of all, for making me laugh.

To Terry Rudolph. You helped me realize that it was okay to be a girl, especially during the awkward years. It was you who sprinkled the magic on our skating career.

To Thelma Wilson for the endless encouragement and support you always gave me. I miss you. The skating world will never be the same without you.

To Mr. Ed Mosler. Your enthusiasm and generosity was and always will be appreciated by all of us. "Yes, I believe in angels."

To Dick Button, the voice of figure skating, thank you for always being fair and kind to Randy and me, even when we weren't at our best.

To Leonard Glussman for the guidance and for putting everything in its proper place. I am forever grateful.

To Dennis Pastor. You picked up where Leonard left off. Thank you for protecting the green stuff! I value your friendship and expertise.

To Ice Capades' George Eby and Dick Palmer for hanging in there with me when I was struggling to find my way in the early 1980s. I would not change a thing.

To Lee Mimms for always making us laugh and teaching us about being respected professionals.

To Sarah Kawahara for helping me to find my wings. Thank you for being so patient.

To Jef Billings for making me feel like a star on and off the ice. You are brilliant! I cherish our wacky and wonderful friendship.

To Michael and Nancy Rosenberg. You have seen me go through it all, often butting heads but always out of love. Thank you for helping Randy and me to take it to the next level. You were wonderful managers.

To Chris Knight. I will always have a special place for you in my heart.

To Stevie Nicks for the gold crescent moon that is so much a part of me, for taking the time to write the Foreword, and for your timeless, magical music.

To Marina (Ma) for being the big sister that I never had. We have seen each other through thick and thin. Our bond will never be broken.

To Harry Langdon for capturing the many sides of Randy and me. I thank you for always making us look beautiful.

To Dick Foster, Cathy and Willy Bietak, and Rick Porter for always believing in Randy and me. I feel blessed to have worked for you.

To Tom Collins. From day one, I always knew you would be the angel who watched over and protected Randy and me. Thank you for allowing us to celebrate our twenty-fifth and thirtieth anniversaries with Champions on Ice. Your extreme generosity will never be forgotten. I adore you!

To Emily Bindiger for being a true and loyal friend through the great and not-so-great times.

To Charles Tentindo (Cha), my wonderful friend and writing partner, you know I will always be there for you.

To Michael Sterling and Todd Frasier for reinventing and always keeping it fun.

To all the "talking doctors" who have sat and listened, a big thank you.

To my dear friends who are on hiatus: Brian Pockar, John Curry, Bruno Jerry, and Robert Wagenhoffer. I know that you'll be back in some way, shape, or form. See you soon.

To Cary Butler for being a wonderful, loving father to our son, Scout. Everything happens for a reason. We created "the rainbow kid."

To Jeff Hull for your love, honesty, support, and patience. Let's keep this growing, now and forever.

To Matt Terry at K.S.A. for being such a wonderful friend and for introducing me to the infomercial world.

To Mark Adelman. I think that we have come full circle. Right on!

To Casa Malibu. Whenever I need to chill, I know where to go.

—Tai Babilonia

To Mom, Dad, and Gordy for everything.

To Jay Gendron for the years of love, support, confidence, and guidance.

To John Nicks for his tireless training and unwavering desire to make us the best we could be.

To Mabel Fairbanks, whose memory influences my life to this day.

To the Babilonia family for their everlasting confidence in everything that we do.

To Tom Collins for his support of our career since the 1970s.

To Willy and Cathy Bietak, who keep hiring us.

To Rick Porter, who keeps hiring us.

To Jola and Tom Berstler for unequaled friendship.

To Michael Sterling for the many years of great publicity and image making.

To Michael and Nancy Rosenberg. Those two are amazing.

To Terry Rudolph for her education in dance, choreography, and style.

To Mark Adelman for helping to start a new chapter.

And to all the others who give me the desire and the will to keep going and who make me smile and laugh every day. These friends are true gems.

—Randy Gardner

Special Acknowledgement

To Martha Kimball for your dedication and endless hours on this project. You believed that it could and should be done. You were a joy to work with. Thanks to you, Randy and I can now share part of our lives with the wonderfully loyal fans who supported us through the years.

Much love and thanks,
Tai

forever two as one

      forced to hold his hand at a very early age
            still today side-by-side atop the frozen stage
      good times bad times
            we've survived them as a team
      to sustain this hidden love we share
            every night I dream
      misfortune in '80 maybe meant to be
            trust and understanding will always be the key
      memories shared as shadows
            the majority of them fun
      when the glow is gone
            we depart still friends . . .
                forever two as one

Tai

july 16, 1984, 4:00 A.M.
p.s. lots of brandy

A Note from Randy

Originally this book was meant to be Tai's and my story told through pictures—thirty years' worth! We began writing and found, as many authors do, that the material kept pouring out. We ended up with more text than photos.

I have found participating in this project with Tai and Martha not only cathartic but also an interesting exercise in self-exploration. Tai and I tried to dig deep to uncover forgotten incidents and facts. Tai remembered more than I did, particularly names and faces.

She and I are skating partners, traveling companions, colleagues, and friends. Our success, first as amateurs and then as a professional skating team, has been extraordinary at the very least. In my opinion, however, that success takes the silver medal compared to our long-lasting friendship. Damn, we've had so much fun along the way!

Summarizing our relationship for others has always been a challenge. I try to simplify my explanation. Instead of doing what some people do alone, I do it with someone else—a partner. We are twins, brother and sister; two, not one; two as one. Tai and Randy.

chapter one

The Frozen Moment

The 1980 U.S. Olympic team: (standing) Michael Seibert, Judy Blumberg, Peter Carruthers, Lisa-Marie Allen, Michael Botticelli, Scott Hamilton, John Summers, Sandy Lenz, Charlie Tickner, Sheryl Franks, Linda Fratianne, Randy, David Santee, Paul George, team leader; (seated) Claire Ferguson, team leader, Tai, Kitty Carruthers, and Stacey Smith.

The Frozen Moment

The French have a phrase for it: Plus ça change, plus c'est la même chose. *The years pass by, but the same situations recur.*

A dramatic pairs competition marked the 2002 Olympic Games in Salt Lake City, Utah. Jamie Salé and David Pelletier of Canada were so closely matched with Russians Elena Berezhnaya and Anton Sikharulidze that their event ultimately ended in a dead heat. The International Skating Union issued two sets of gold medals. Apart from the judging scandal that precipitated such an unprecedented action, valid arguments could be made on behalf of each team—although the arguments on behalf of the North Americans were generally considered more convincing.

Twenty-two years ago two other pairs teams, one North American and one Russian, were just as evenly matched. If the outcome of their rivalry was not the same, public feelings ran just as high.

In late January of 1980 the idyllic and supremely ambitious Adirondack hamlet of Lake Placid, New York, winter population 2,997, waited with joy and trepidation to welcome the world. Across the continent in a suburb of Los Angeles, California, twenty-two-year-old Randy Gardner experienced the same potent blend of contradictory emotions. One-half of the reigning world champion figure skating pairs team, co-favorite for Olympic gold, he had just stepped into a double flip and ripped the adductor muscle in his left thigh and groin.

Randy and his lifelong skating partner, twenty-year-old Tai Babilonia, planned to leave for Lake Placid in less than two weeks. The Opening Ceremonies were scheduled for February 13, followed two days later by the pairs short program event. A young man of few words and fewer complaints, Randy kept his fears to himself, as he bottled up so much else in his life, hiding it all beneath a cheerful, optimistic exterior. His injury was "skateable," so he trained in pain.

As a result of intense press coverage and biases born of cultural differences and international politics, the hopes of an entire nation rested on Tai and Randy's sturdy yet vulnerable shoulders. In winning their 1979 world title, they had interrupted fourteen years of Soviet domination in the pairs event. Years five through fourteen of that era belonged to a doe-eyed Russian dynamo, Irina Rodnina, whose maternity leave in the fifteenth season coincided with Babilonia and Gardner's apotheosis.

In that era when Glasnost was unimaginable, an American pair had never won Olympic gold. Newspaper scribes and network moguls hungrily contemplated the showdown in Lake Placid.

Babilonia and Gardner's appeal transcended nationalism. In a sport of "one-and-one-half" pairs, tall, mature men linked with prepubescent girls capable of effortless twists and throws but little artistry, Tai and Randy were equals in every way, flowing into tandem spirals, spreadeagles, and spins.

Without sentimentalizing it or even analyzing its nature, they had formed a bond of unquestioning loyalty and subliminal communication that translated into ethereal fluidity. In little more than an Olympiad they had grown from long-legged adolescents with braces on their teeth into refined masters of matched interpretive movement. If the skating world was charmed, the press was besotted.

Those were the pressures that weighed upon Randy one bone-chilling day in a Santa Monica ice rink when a chain of events that changed two lives lurched into motion.

Tai and I were doing a run-through of our Olympic short program when I went up into the double flip jump. As I pulled in with my legs, I could feel one of my groin muscles strain. I had suffered adductor injuries before—on both sides of my body—but they hadn't proven serious. The pain of the new injury seemed tolerable, so I didn't say much about it. Tai and I finished our normal practice session.

Later I iced the aching muscle. My doctor gave me anti-inflammatory medication so that Tai and I could continue our daily training. I don't remember being unduly worried or upset about the injury. We were so excited about the upcoming Olympics in Lake Placid, so focused on preparing to compete, all the while trying to ignore the turmoil that swirled around us as we skated in the eye of a hurricane.

There is such a monumental buildup, so much emphasis on winning the Olympics. Members of the press declare you victorious even before you arrive at the venue. Heaven forbid that you should receive the silver medal as Michelle Kwan did in Nagano. It's almost as though silver doesn't count.

All that Randy and I wanted to do was skate our best—a cliché, but true for us. Whatever was meant to happen would happen. The networks and the print media were so powerful, but they didn't understand what an athlete went through just to *get* to the Olympics, just to *qualify*.

It was unsettling to walk into newsstands and see our pictures everywhere. The captions were always "America's Hopefuls for the Gold." We hadn't left for Lake Placid. We weren't even *there* yet. We were still running our number because I couldn't get through the whole long program without an error. And I was five pounds overweight, even though I probably hadn't eaten all day, and I was hungry. You have to be tough to block out the press coverage. I've seen it tear people apart.

The "heated rivalry" between Randy and me and the pair of Irina Rodnina and Aleksandr Zaitsev was just a media invention. The Soviet team was the last thing on our minds. Randy and I were entirely focused on preparing to get through our own short and long programs successfully. The media trumped up the rest of the story to boost readership and television ratings.

Rodnina and Zaitsev were so much older than we were, and Irina was in a league by herself. I admired her tremendously. Her previous partner, Alexsei Ulanov, had unceremoniously dumped her after their 1972 Olympic and world gold medal victories in order to pair up with his new love interest, Ludmila Smirnova. *Switching partners and continuing to win! How did Irina do that?* She was an amazing athlete. I never watched *him*. No one did. You only watched her.

Publicity crews filming at the rink during our training sessions were a constant distraction. Several times I walked off the ice crying. Spotlights blinded us. We had pieces of equipment strapped around us. Microphones picked up everything that we said. That interrupted our focus at a crucial time. I knew that the intrusion wasn't fair, but we were powerless to stop it.

The Frozen Moment

The people at *Us* magazine decided to do a day-in-the-life feature. They followed Randy and me to the rink to watch us train with our coach, John Nicks, and work at the barre with our ballet teacher, Terry Rudolph. Then they wanted to show us having fun, so they asked us to go out on a double date. I had never been on a date before. Randy, though he sometimes dated, didn't have a steady girlfriend. We really had to scramble for a couple of days to come up with partners.

Randy ended up escorting Mr. Nicks's daughter, Kim. One of my friends, Linda Haack, conveniently had an available cousin, a gorgeous football player. I don't remember who

Irina Rodnina and Aleksandr Zaitsev in 1978. (Mike Cosgrove)

called whom, but he agreed to drive to my house in the San Fernando Valley to pick me up just like a real date. I was so nervous. I didn't know what to wear or what to say.

I had never met the guy before. I'm not quite sure whether or not he knew anything at all about figure skating, let alone about Randy and me, but he thought that the whole idea was great. He enjoyed himself.

Our date consisted of going to see a show starring Eartha Kitt somewhere in Hollywood. I believe that it was called *Timbuktu*. The four of us met at the theater and saw the play. Then the *Us* photographer joined us afterward at a restaurant.

I don't remember saying anything to the gorgeous football player. I don't even know whether or not I *looked* at him. In the magazine photo we seem to be having a great time, but I really had no idea how to act. He drove me home and kissed me on the cheek. I probably broke a sweat over that. I never heard from him again. I guess that I was pretty boring.

Dating for Us magazine.

The Frozen Moment

When the magazine came out, the photo caption read, "Double Dates Are the Only Time Babilonia and Gardner Take Different Partners." We found that extremely humorous.

The evening felt every bit as staged as it was. *Us* magazine was clearly hyping Tai and me as America's sweethearts. That was fine. It could have been worse.

People always presumed that we were boyfriend and girlfriend, husband and wife, or brother and sister. I suppose that it was natural for the public to think of us as a couple. Our names were so closely connected. There was never a hint of romantic attachment between us, however. In some ways our connection was much more profound.

When the time came to leave for Lake Placid, my family, Tai's family, and Mr. Nicks all went on the same flight. The desk clerk who checked us in at the American Airlines counter at LAX upgraded the whole group to first class, compliments of the airline, a luxury that we certainly couldn't have afforded to pay for.

Tai and I kept each other entertained on airplanes. She boarded with six or seven magazines under her arm and read them throughout the flight, giggling and pointing out silly little things that amused her. That got me laughing, too. It helped pass the time. Tai is a great one for the lurid enticements of the *Star* or the *National Enquirer*.

We flew into Albany, New York, on a jet, then took a commuter plane to the tiny Lake Placid airport that consisted of a small house and a runway. When we reached the Olympic Village, we Americans were assigned to trailer-like structures on the Village grounds. Mine had four bedrooms and two baths. I shared it with David Santee, a men's competitor, Michael Botticelli, a pairs skater, and John Summers, an ice dancer. Tai had a little room in a similar trailer with Sheryl Franks, Michael's partner.

It was fun for us to walk around the Village and get to know some of the other athletes. We met skiers Steve and Phil Mahre, speed skater Eric Heiden, and hockey players Jim Craig and Mike Eruzione, who later achieved the upset of the century by defeating the Soviet Union.

Tai and I had a few days of practice before the Olympics officially began. On the day of the Opening Ceremonies all the athletes were taken to the venue and made to sit for what seemed like hours in a long line of buses. I remember the thrill of finally walking into the stadium, seeing the crowd, and especially *hearing* the crowd. There was such enthusiasm, such overwhelming applause, when the American team walked in behind Scott Hamilton, the elected U.S. flag bearer and a friend of ours. Scott, a men's competitor, was dating our friend and fellow pairs skater Kitty Carruthers at the time.

Tai and I had a practice session that night in the brand new rink at the Olympic Centre in the heart of Lake Placid Village. Four or five pairs teams darted across the ice, dodging each other. Tai and I were working on our long program when I went up into the air in a double Axel and felt something pull. It was my adductor muscle again and this time my hip flexor, too. That really scared me. The pain shot right up through my abdomen. Canadian skating champion Elvis Stojko suffered from the identical injury during the 1998 Olympics. I felt for him.

Mr. Nicks and I walked to the United States Olympic Committee's Olympic Village medical facility where the team physician, orthopedic surgeon Dr. Anthony Daly of Inglewood, California, treated my injury with ice, ultrasound, and Jacuzzi therapy. Dr. Daly said very little at that point. He didn't offer a prognosis, and I didn't ask for one. I suspect that I was afraid to hear the worst.

Tai knew, of course, that I had aggravated my training injury, but she wasn't aware of how serious the situation was. *I* truly didn't know. I knew only that it hurt. Mr. Nicks, a Briton with a stiff upper lip, didn't seem outwardly concerned, but I'm sure that he worried. We all plowed through our routines as though life was normal. Meanwhile our subconscious minds churned.

We had a practice session on February 15, the day of the short program event. The competition was scheduled for 9:00 P.M. As was our custom at event-day practices, we skipped the full run-through, but we tested each individual element: side-by-side double flips, a backward inside death spiral, a one-arm star lift, side-by-side change sit spins, a catch-camel pairs spin, and a serpentine step sequence.

I felt wobbly when I lifted Tai. The pain became acute. Mr. Nicks and I decided that the only choice I had was to numb the injury. I was in too much pain to skate without some help. Tai was left out of the decision-making process.

I rested for a while. Then Tai and I left for the arena early so that Dr. Daly could administer my shot. On the way we noticed that the managers of the Golden Arrow, the hotel opposite the Olympic Centre, had put up a big good luck sign for us. We appreciated the gesture, but we were going to need a lot more than luck.

Dr. Daly and a female therapist took me to a private locker room fifteen minutes before the start of the pairs short program event. I received three c.c.s of Xylocaine and went into one of the two smaller rinks in the Olympic Centre complex to test the drug's effects. So far, so good.

Then Tai and I went to the backstage area of the main rink to do our regular floor warm-ups and stretches. I felt pretty comfortable. The pain had subsided by then. I crossed my fingers that I would be able to go out onto the on-ice warm-up and do what I needed to do, but I soon found to my shock that the Xylocaine had numbed too wide an area.

Scott Hamilton

I remember the Lake Placid setting well. There was the formal, permanent part of the Olympic Village that later became a prison, but all the people I knew on the American team and even some of the coaches were in modular, prefabricated temporary housing. The units were like the buildings that are put up on construction sites to house offices. There were four bedrooms and two bathrooms in each half of one of those units. The walls were really thin, and the bedrooms were tiny. There was nothing glamorous. It was just enough to sustain life for a while. However, there were generous public areas in the Village. In particular, the game room was fun, and there was a theater where concerts took place. The cafeteria was a good size, too.

I knew that Randy was nursing an injury, but I didn't know how serious it was. The pairs event was first, and I was spending most of my time hanging out with Kitty Carruthers, another pairs competitor. A lot of information, too, remained secret. The fact that even Tai wasn't really kept informed of Randy's medical situation reveals a great deal about the level of secrecy that was maintained.

The Frozen Moment

Dr. Daly later told the press that the shot was "mostly for show" to help me mentally block out the pain. The three c.c.s constituted too small a dose, in his opinion, to have caused such numbness. I found that hard to believe. When I skated out onto the ice, I couldn't pull in to rotate. I couldn't control my jumps. I felt weird. My balance was off, especially in the star lift. That was dangerous for Tai.

Of the required elements in the short program—one double jump, one lift, one footwork sequence, one death spiral, and two spins—I couldn't complete three out of six.

I realized that Randy couldn't skate without some pain relief. Although no one consulted me about using Xylocaine, at least I knew about the shot. I presumed that Randy would be okay. None of us suspected that the numbness would spread the way it eventually did.

Randy and Mr. Nicks were two tight-lipped stoics. They didn't discuss the situation with me as it developed. I went onto the warm-up believing that everything was under control. We would skate for a chance at the gold medal.

Randy and I had drawn to compete fourth of the twelve teams. That meant that we were last in the first warm-up group. Just before I stepped onto the ice with the rest of Group One, Mr. Nicks told me to take off my necklace. He was afraid that it would get caught in the rows of rhinestones on my costume, and he didn't want anything to distract me. I did not want to remove my good luck charm. It had come to me in a very special way, and I never took it off.

One day during the summer of 1979 Randy and I received a message that the well-known singer Stevie Nicks (no relation to our coach) wanted to stop by the rink to give us some gifts. *No way! This has to be a prank.*

The appointed hour passed, and we continued to wait for some time for Stevie to arrive. Eventually we left and went home, sure that someone had played a practical joke on us. Half an hour later, according to Mr. Nicks's secretary, Stevie appeared in her platform boots, with red chiffon swirling everywhere, bearing programs and T-shirts from her last Fleetwood Mac tour and a gold moon pendant for me.

Stevie had written a song called "Sisters of the Moon," and she gave the crescents to people she loved and admired. She was a ballet and figure skating fan, and somehow she felt a deep connection to Randy and me.

I always did what Mr. Nicks told me to do, so I handed him the necklace. He held it for me while Randy and I skated out onto the ice.

Randy is the leader of our team. I have always taken my cues from him. That night in Lake Placid I became the leader. I was the one in control. From that fact alone I deduced that something was terribly wrong.

Ordinarily Randy *does not fall*, but he simply could not land his double flip jump. He fell twice while attempting it.

"Try a sit spin," Mr. Nicks told him.

His leg buckled, and he fell again. That was the moment when the eighty-five hundred people in the audience let out a collective gasp of shock and horror. I gasped right along with them.

The warm-up ended then. Mr. Nicks told us in his matter-of-fact voice that we would try our elements again when our turn came to compete. We left the ice to wait. While the three teams ahead of us skated—the West Germans, the East Germans, and the British pair—Tai and I went backstage and sat on chairs in the concrete hallway. We went through the usual motions to keep limber and prepare ourselves psychologically. The wait was nerve-wracking. We didn't talk to each other.

As the announcer read the marks of Susan Garland and Robert Daw, Tai and I skated around in a small oval to get the feel of the ice. I tried the double flip again and fell.

That fall was the most devastating of all. The situation seemed simply unbelievable. I felt as though I had slid into a trance. Everything from that moment on assumed a dreamlike air of unreality.

At competitions I always knew where my mother was sitting. When Randy fell for the last time, I looked up at her in the audience. Then I shrugged in confusion.

Mr. Nicks called us off the ice. He spoke to our team leader and manager, Paul George, who walked around to the referee and delivered the message that soon boomed from the public address system: Ladies and gentlemen, Tai Babilonia and Randy Gardner will be unable to compete at this time due to injury.

The competition went on without us.

Randy has never watched that episode on videotape. Twenty-two years later it's still too painful for him. I have seen it several times, and it *is* a hard thing to watch. The ABC commentator, Dick Button, became emotional. He shed a few tears. I could hear them in his voice.

When Mr. Nicks returned my necklace, I put it right back around my neck. I haven't gone a day since then without wearing at least the charm. If the chain catches on my clothes, or if I want to wear a different necklace, I take the moon off the chain and pin it inside my bodice.

Randy returned immediately to the private locker room where Dr. Daly had given him the injection. He was hemorrhaging internally, and his skin was turning black and blue. While the doctor and the therapist iced the strained muscles, Mr. Gardner arrived. Randy was still stunned.

Meanwhile skating officials sheltered me from crowds of concerned people. The Pinkerton's guards in their big Mountie hats somehow got me out of the arena. Walking from the backstage area to a waiting car was a major ordeal. There was mayhem all around me. I remember the press swarming like bees, but I didn't talk to any of the reporters that night. There was a team house where the American athletes were allowed to hang out, eat, and relax during their free time. Someone took me straight there, and Randy joined me a little while later.

Eventually Claire Ferguson, the assistant American team leader, ushered me outside to a waiting car. The United States Figure Skating Association (USFSA) had determined that the team house was the safest place for Tai and me to go because the officials there could control who passed in and out. We attempted—I don't know why—to watch the rest of the pairs competition on television. We sat in chairs in front of the TV, just staring straight ahead. We were both in a daze. Paparazzi came to the door, but our parents and team leaders locked us inside and stood guard.

The other people in the team house were just as sad as Tai and I, so the atmosphere was quiet and heavy—as though a member of the family had died and friends had gathered to lend support. In a sense that was the case. Our amateur career had quite suddenly died. People were there for us, but there wasn't much that they could say or do to make things better.

As I watched the other pairs' performances on television, the images went right through me. Nothing sank in. I was depressed, scared, and locked on autopilot.

After the telecast ended, I went to the house my family had rented for their stay in Lake Placid. My paternal grandmother was there with my father, Connie, my brother, Constancio, and some friends. I don't believe that I cried.

Constancio and I sat down and began to talk about our childhood. We had never done that before. Maybe he started the conversation just because he sensed that I needed an outlet. We laughed together. *Do you remember the time . . .* I was venting, I guess. We didn't discuss anything skating-related. I bottled that up. That night I stayed with my parents instead of returning to the Olympic Village. I managed to sleep for a few hours.

I went to my parents' hotel and spent a restless night there. My injuries hurt, and the phone calls kept pouring in: from the Los Angeles press, from various sportscasters we knew, and from some friends of ours. People also came and knocked on the door. We didn't have a publicist there to run interference for us, something that many skaters have today. I spoke to a few of the friends who phoned. Tai and I were told later that President Carter had tried to get through to us.

Linda Fratianne

I wasn't allowed to go to any of the Olympic events because the ladies' competition was last. I had heard about Randy's problem, so I was glued to the pairs on television in my hotel room. I saw Randy fall on the double flip. When Tai burst into tears, I lost it, too. My mother was at the arena, and I remember sitting in our room crying all by myself. I felt so bad. I thought, "All the time and all the talent going into this pair, and they don't get to skate!" It was devastating to me and, I am sure, devastating to people all across the country and the world.

With President and Mrs. Carter in the White House.

When I woke up the next morning, I was in a fog. I didn't know what I was doing. I didn't know where to go. Tai felt confused as well. Mr. Nicks told us that we had to give a press conference.

What bothered us most was that we didn't know what the public thought about the situation. Were people angry with us? Had we let everyone down? I assumed that I had disappointed our skating fans, our families, and all our fellow members of the U.S. figure skating team. I also felt guilty about Tai.

It didn't occur to us, though, to share our feelings with one another. Randy never said, "Tai, I'm sorry about what happened." I never asked him, "Are you okay? How are you feeling? Did the shot sting?" Nothing! Oddly enough, twenty-two years later, we still haven't had that conversation.

I would love to bring up the subject, but I believe that the first move is Randy's. When he is ready, we will talk about Lake Placid. It is obvious to me that he is not ready yet, and I can understand that. Our minds work in different ways. Randy likes to keep the waters smooth. I am just the opposite these days.

At that point in our lives we were programmed and dedicated as athletes. Much of our failure to communicate, I realize now, was due to denial. We were trying to move on to the next thing, and we avoided attacking the issues that we should have addressed. Tai and I maintained a surface relationship, even though we loved each other as friends. We didn't have deep discussions. Tai was concerned and supportive, though. She often came into the clinic when I was with Dr. Daly and asked him how I was doing.

Someone offered to go back to the Olympic Village for us the next morning. Outside our doors were stacks of telegrams—hundreds of them. Ultimately the number of messages reached ten thousand. The boxes were brought to our press conference in the auditorium of Lake Placid High School. We sat there reading telegrams to the three hundred assembled journalists. Singer Rosemary Clooney's happened to be one of the first telegrams that we picked up, but the messages came from anyone and everyone.

Those telegrams helped us to get through the day. We suddenly realized that people understood. They had been through things like this, too. They knew that we were human. We had real muscles. Anything could happen. Our fans still loved us. Many of them expressed the same thought: "You have won the gold in our hearts."

It was a tough press conference, though. The reporters were sensitive to our feelings. There was nothing rude or out of line. But there were *so many* reporters, and they threw every imaginable question at us. I went into the bathroom afterward and cried.

Lisa-Marie Allen

Way back when all of us were young skaters, we were not taught to communicate. Everything was so competitive and private. The issues took on disproportionate drama and importance. We followed everybody's orders, so we didn't learn the technique of thinking on our own. At the ripe age of thirty-something we all suddenly realized, "Wow, I have an opinion, and I'm allowed to voice it."

One day I ran into Tai in the housewares department at Macy's. We talked for forty-five minutes—about things that, in twenty years' time, we had never talked about before, like the Olympics and what happened to her and Randy there. I said, "You know, Tai, I can't express the horror and sadness that most of your teammates felt, and we couldn't even be there for you."

None of us who stayed in the Village—at least I can speak for myself—knew that Randy was injured. Because we had to be up early the next day, we watched the pairs short program in the lounge on a big-screen TV. After Tai and Randy's withdrawal, they were whisked away. We didn't have the chance to express our sorrow about what had happened to them. We couldn't even say, "Goodbye. I'm sorry. I'll skate my heart out for you."

In the rumor mill there was very disturbing [and false] speculation that Mr. Nicks might have withdrawn Tai and Randy because he thought that they couldn't win. I had ten days to go before my event started, and to have that thought lingering in the back of my head was uncomfortable. There was no closure.

The next time I saw them was when they came through town with Ice Capades. Over the years we never touched on the subject. It wasn't really "touchable." But I finally had that chance, nearly twenty years later in Macy's, to tell Tai how horrible I had felt about the Olympics.

Later the same day Randy and I and our four parents had a meeting with Mr. Nicks to figure out what to do next. The atmosphere was tense, to say the least. During that heated gathering, Randy's mother blurted out a tragic piece of news that my father had been keeping secret until he could find the right moment to break it to us gently: Mom's mother was dead. She had just passed away back in California. What a horrible way for us to find out!

What else could go wrong? I didn't have to wait long to find out. Someone had spoken to the *National Enquirer*, claiming that the reason Randy was injured was that I was overweight. That comment, as shocking and hurtful as it was, truly affected me throughout the rest of my skating career. I began to doubt and blame myself when there was no rational basis for self-blame. Although I was trim and in excellent shape, that seed of insecurity took root. I later was shocked when I learned the source of the comment, and it took me a long time to forgive her. At some point, though, you do have to forgive.

While Randy and I were still living in the Olympic Village, elementary school children began sending us letters, some of the funniest drawings of us, and little medals made of paper or foil. Those were priceless! I still have all of them. That humorous and touching show of support was what got us through the rest of the Olympics. Then we knew that everything would be okay.

The situation had been scary for us, though. We knew how many people had watched us on television, but we hadn't dared guess their reactions. *What can they be thinking? Do they feel sorry for us? Are they upset that we let them down?* We finally knew the answers when we read our mail. The public reaction was pure love.

John Nicks

My memory of Lake Placid is very clear. Randy had suffered a bad groin injury approximately two to three weeks before the winter Olympics, had been given treatment by a variety of medical advisors, and hadn't improved a lot. During that time Randy and I had agreed not to disclose fully to Tai the severity of the injury, because she worried about him a lot. The injury was not publicized. That was a political decision that I made.

We got to Lake Placid, and it became apparent that Randy could not compete in that situation at all. He kept on hoping that it was going to get better. Medical advice said it *should* get better, but it really didn't. The only option we had on the day of the competition was to take some more medical advice and arrange for a painkilling injection to be done prior to the competition by Dr. Anthony Daly, who was the chief medical officer of the United States Olympic team in Lake Placid. The doctor gave Randy the shot in one of the hockey change rooms approximately half an hour before the competition. Immediately after that injection was made, Randy told me that the pain had decreased substantially and he felt much better. We were all feeling good at that time.

Tai and Randy went on the ice to warm up. It immediately became clear to me—and to Randy—that although the pain had gone, a lot of control and strength had gone, too. He began missing double flips, which were extremely easy for him.

Then he started lifting Tai. The mandatory lift was a one-armed star in which Tai was over his head, inverted in a perpendicular position with her head toward the ice. The very first time they did it, he obviously had a weakness in the groin and collapsed in the middle of the lift. It was very lucky that Tai didn't suffer a severe injury. She came down quickly, and Randy half saved her. It was extremely dangerous. All of this was happening in the course of three or four minutes.

Randy went back to try the double flip again, and it didn't work. I really at that point had no option but to

There was some talk of us leaving early, getting out of Lake Placid, but then we were notified that President Jimmy Carter had invited the entire American team to fly to Washington, D.C., to meet with him and the First Lady, Rosalyn, on the day after the Closing Ceremonies. Tai and I decided to stay on.

David Santee, Michael Botticelli, and Linda Fratianne, the U.S. ladies' champion who won a silver medal in Lake Placid, all tried to cheer me up. I even danced with Irina Rodnina in the Village disco. I don't believe that I spent much time with Tai during the remainder of the Games. She was busy running after Eric Heiden.

I developed a huge crush on Eric, the speed skater who won five gold medals in Lake Placid. I got together with one of my friends, Liz Cain, an Australian pairs skater who trained with Randy and me in Santa Monica. She and I stalked Eric—in our own charming, innocent way. I was an Eric Heiden groupie.

Because the pairs competition had been early in the event schedule and because Randy wasn't around, I had a lot of idle time. Liz and I hung out and watched Eric race. He was so cute. His body looked incredible in that sleek, golden speed skating suit of his. He kept winning gold medals as if the effort were nothing. He would win one, take a day off, then go out and win another. It was amazing.

After each gold-medal victory Eric hosted a party in his room in the Olympic Village for all of his speed skating friends. Liz and I, though uninvited, somehow always ended up at the party. We were in awe of Eric, and he was so sweet to us. He was a very nice guy.

withdraw them for two reasons. First, he couldn't complete the elements that he had to. But more importantly, there was a great danger to Tai, particularly during the twist and the lifts that they would perform.

There was, of course, a lot of media attention. The withdrawal was a shock to everybody in the building. I remember going in front of a press conference that evening that must have included at least two hundred media representatives. I did have the good sense to ask the doctor to accompany me. He responded to most of the questions, which were medical. By the time that was over—it took an hour—Tai and Randy had left. I didn't see them anymore that night. I called them but was unable to get to them because the phone lines were very busy. I didn't talk to them until the next day.

I must say that, although of course it was calamitous, very shortly they began to feel a lot better because of the extraordinary amount of mail and public response they got: wooden golden medals, pictures, animals, cards—between six and eight thousand pieces of mail within seventy-two hours.

It was very disappointing to be with two wonderful young skaters for that number of years, to have the opportunity to win Olympic gold, and for it not to happen. But I have somewhat of a pragmatic nature, and so I just moved on. They'd had a wonderful career. They were world champions. I believe that they were just as successful professionally as if they had won the gold.

I do remember watching the other co-favorites. They skated well. It would have been a good competition. Rodnina and her partner were probably superior in athleticism. Tai and Randy were certainly superior from the artistic side. I think that Tai and Randy would have won because they were younger, they were the reigning world champions, and they had brought a different style—a very balletic, artistic style—back into pairs skating the previous year. It had been well received by the skating establishment and the judges, so I think that they had the edge if they had skated well. But who knows?

Months later, when Randy and I played Long Beach during our Ice Capades opening, my mother and I stayed in a hotel near the arena because it was a little too far for us to drive from home every day. One night after the show, Mom and I were in our hotel room watching *The Tonight Show*. Eric Heiden happened to be a guest on the program. When Johnny Carson asked him to name a highlight of his Olympic experience, Eric announced, "Partying with Tai Babilonia."

I fell on the floor! At first I was shocked because Eric had thought to mention me. Then I was shocked because my *mother* was sitting beside me.

When our Ice Capades company eventually reached Washington, D.C., we presented our 1979 long program costumes to the Smithsonian Institution National Museum of American History. The curators displayed them alongside some Peggy Fleming memorabilia and Eric Heiden's sleek, golden speed skating suit. I found that so very poetic.

I don't remember seeing some of our skating friends at all during the Olympics— Linda Fratianne, Scott Hamilton, or Lisa-Marie Allen. It wasn't that our families and team officials continued to keep Randy and me sheltered. It was just that the overlapping timing of all the practices and events made socializing difficult. Occasionally I saw a member of my team in one of the housing units.

My Olympics ended on a somber note. For some reason I didn't have a reserved seat for the Closing Ceremonies, although my athlete's pass admitted me to the arena. I was alone. I climbed all the way to the top of the stands and found someone with an extra seat. I sat there and watched the ceremonies with tears streaming down my face. A tangle of emotions rose to the surface, melted down my cheeks, and dripped onto my USA team jacket. I don't remember leaving the arena and returning to the Village that night. It's all a blur.

Robin Cousins

When it came together for Tai and Randy in 1979— the year when it fell apart for lots of other people—it really was a magical moment. Until then the Soviets and East Germans had been the dominant force in pairs skating. When Tai and Randy showed that they were more than capable of ousting Rodnina and Zaitsev, they were suddenly expected to become the next Olympic champions. Then Rodnina and Zaitsev came back. I don't know that there was ever going to be an objective look at the two teams if both skated perfectly.

I was quite torn. For me Rodnina was one of the greatest people who ever put foot on the ice because of the depth of her knowledge of her craft and her complete understanding of what the blade did and what skating was all about. On the other hand, there was a pleasing linear quality to Tai and Randy's skating. Nothing was rushed. Even the fast steps and tricks flowed smoothly. There never seemed to be a lot of energy expended, though you knew there had to be;

whereas the Russians were like thoroughbred racehorses, and that does *get* to you. The two pairs were chalk and cheese.

I was in the Olympic arena on the night of the short program. It was *Bambi*. I know that's a silly way to put it, but the way I recall watching the warm-up, every time Randy jumped, it was the movie *Bambi* all over again. There wasn't a crash. There was just a leg buckling underneath and a body flopping to the floor. I remember the disbelief—or the realization, or both—on Tai's face when it ended.

As strong, efficient, and emotional as Rodnina and Zaitsev were, I don't recall their performance as historical. I do think, though, that people felt that the skating world had been robbed of a truly historical confrontation, and the *what if* question mark was never removed.

When you realize something like that, you start unknowingly to compensate. Every performance becomes

I went to physical therapy three times a day, so I didn't see many of the competitions. I didn't attend any skating events at all because I just didn't want to be around the sport. Although I saw the U.S. team win the gold medal in ice hockey, I can't say that I truly enjoyed the Olympics. I felt out of place. My balloon had popped and shriveled.

I wasn't bitter, though. I was extremely happy to learn that I would be able to continue to skate once my groin and hip muscles healed. One of my greatest secret fears had been that the injuries would end our professional career before it began. Not to be physically able to do what you want most to do is a frightening thing, especially for an athlete. Fortunately Tai and I would be able to turn pro and start a new facet of our skating life. We had never planned to remain amateur after Lake Placid.

I do sometimes wonder what would have happened if we had been able to compete. We might have won if we had skated perfectly. Rodnina and Zaitsev didn't perform as well as usual. They were relatively slow. Irina had given birth to their baby, Sasha, some eleven months earlier. Besides, there would have been a huge crowd reaction in our favor. The judges would have felt the heat of the North American audience.

There was such an overwhelming response to our disappointment. Perhaps we were better off than had we competed and won. We will never know, but in many ways I believe that.

We gained a lot of fans because of Lake Placid. They embraced us—and still do, even today. We're pretty lucky. I don't know whether or not the fans would have reacted as kindly if we had won.

the *what if* performance. That is a devastating position to be put in. Throughout all their subsequent years of Ice Capades, all their years of being true stars, Tai and Randy were the "hard-luck kids." It makes me sick every time I see the media do that to athletes who have had a rough championship. It was hard luck only that they didn't get to do one event. Look at everything else that they have accomplished. People assume so much about the Olympics. If it had been the other way around, if they hadn't won the world championship, nobody would remember.

But the media love to draw attention to failure, and the "hard luck kids" tag hung around like a noose far longer than it should have.

Tai, I always thought, was one of the sweetest, one of the most lovely, trusting people. If the Olympics had a greater negative impact on her than they did on Randy, perhaps there is a reason. If you know in the back of your mind that something is probably not

going to happen, you have already set yourself up for what will then follow; whereas, if you know nothing, there is suddenly a chasm. Whether or not Randy knew for sure that he wouldn't be able to skate, his mind would have geared itself to that particular *what if* situation. For Tai, stepping onto the ice, there had been no *what if*.

It is a question of perspective, but you're not in a position to say, "Hey, you know what? We have had time to think about it." The one thing that you are never given is the time to think. I have always said that after a world championship or the Olympics—a disaster or a win— you need the whole world to stop. You need to go home, close the door, and get things in perspective. *Okay, now I'm ready. Turn the world back on*. Then off you go. Eventually you are given that time, but by then it may be almost too late.

My mother always told me that everything happens for a reason. I truly believe that some power from above called the shots. Randy and I had won Worlds the year before with the best performance of our amateur career. It was just about perfect. Looking back now, I doubt that we could have topped that performance.

Some people disagree with my cosmic take on the situation. Still I feel in my heart that a higher power put us through some kind of test in Lake Placid. If Randy and I could get through that incredibly difficult night in front of millions of people, we can get through anything in life.

We traveled straight from Lake Placid to Washington, D.C. Meeting President and Mrs. Carter was like spending time with our grandparents. They were so down-home and humble, as though we had known them forever. We've met half a dozen presidents, but Jimmy and Rosalyn Carter impressed us the most. She was particularly nice. You could actually have a normal conversation with her.

The Carters greeted the entire 1980 U.S. Olympic team outside the White House. Then each team member had the chance to be photographed with them in the Blue Room. That visit to the White House was a special way to end our Olympics and our lives as amateur skaters.

chapter two

One and One Make a Pair

I was born Lawrence Randolph Gardner in Los Angeles, California, on December 2, 1957. Since everyone called me Randy virtually from the moment of my birth, I eventually changed my full legal name to Randy Gardner.

My mother, Janice Althea Baker, known as Jan, was a Los Angeles native who met my father, Jack Gardner, when they were students at the University of Southern California. He came from the microscopic hamlet of New England, North Dakota. Dickinson, population sixteen thousand, was the nearest thing to a major city in the area.

My paternal grandparents owned a winter home in Oceanside, a community south of Los Angeles near the San Diego County line. They returned each spring to the North Dakota countryside, where my family frequently visited them during summer vacations.

I had an idyllic *Wonder Years* sort of childhood, growing up at 5829 Chariton Avenue in an area of greater Los Angeles called Ladera Heights, located between Culver City and Inglewood. It was a great little neighborhood: safe, suburban, and middle class. With my many neighborhood friends I walked or rode my bicycle to school and played in the streets until all hours of the night. I wish that there were more neighborhoods like that one today, especially here in the Los Angeles area.

My family always had pets. Ziggy, our brown dachshund, and Barney the beagle both enjoyed exceptionally long life spans. Later I had a dog I called Nicksy in honor of my coach, John Nicks. There were plenty of goldfish, guppies, hamsters, rabbits, and guinea pigs to keep the dogs company in our menagerie. When I look back now, I think, "My poor parents!"

My father worked as an accountant at the Hughes Aircraft Company. My mother was a schoolteacher. She began her career in junior high and high school but spent the largest part of her working life teaching second grade, which she loved. Room 6 at Cowan Avenue Elementary School in Westchester was my mother's domain for a good many years.

My grandmother, my mother's mother, often took care of me while my parents worked. Her name was Eunice Genevieve Baker, although for some reason my brother and I called her Lommie. Her husband, my grandfather, died before I was born.

Lommie lived half an hour away from us. Whenever she came to my house during the week, we played school. I was the teacher. I remember making poor Lommie do writing lessons. She was such a good sport. Sometimes she persuaded my mother to allow me to play hooky and stay home with her, a secret vice that I really enjoyed.

My mother's sister, Aunt Ducky (as we called her) had no children of her own. She maintained piles of scrapbooks recording my wide range of activities and accomplishments. In early 1964 she noted this incident:

"Randy had to stay after school because the teacher said he talked all day—to himself.

With Aunt Ducky.

In our side yard on Chariton Avenue.

My third birthday.

My baby picture.

Making faces at the mall.

Christmas 1961.

With my parents, Jack and Jan, and my brother, Gordy.

Lommie asked Randy what he was talking about. Randy replied, 'I was telling myself I can't do this work.'"

Two years later, when I was eight, I had apparently developed more confidence. Again as reported by my faithful Aunt Ducky, I was repairing my small blackboard when Lommie asked, "Randy, have you ever thought of becoming a schoolteacher like your mommy?"

I assured her, "Why, I could teach first grade right now if they would let me."

Thirty-five years later I finally got my chance at the teaching profession. I instructed a recreational figure skating course at UCLA.

Aside from teaching Lommie, I didn't generally like to be in charge. I wasn't an aggressive child, from what I remember. I was ambitious, though, and rambunctious, always physically active.

I watched dancing on television, on the omnipresent variety shows of the 1960s, and I thought that it was something that I would like to learn to do. I began ballet and tap lessons at the age of six or seven. I still recall being able to feel the music and move to it in rhythm. That is what later attracted me to skating as well.

My mother sometimes brought rhythm band instruments home from school. One that I particularly enjoyed, a miniature harp-like invention, had keys for me to play and strings to strum. At elementary school we had drum pads that we practiced on before the teachers would allow us to use the full-size drums. Then I began accordion lessons and got my own instrument. I couldn't read music well. During recitals I pretended to play while the other students' more melodious sounds covered up whatever noise I made.

Once I started skating, the music lessons stopped. However, I continued to love listening to music, especially movie soundtracks and show scores. My family went to musical films like *The Sound of Music* and *Mary Poppins*. (I was a big fan of Julie Andrews and still am.) Then my parents bought the soundtrack, and I reenacted the movie—my own abbreviated version—in our living room.

That living room was the setting for productions that I mounted with the assistance of Annette and Carol, friends my age who lived across the street. There was always music involved. We danced, played instruments, and pretended to sing. I recall performing enthusiastically to Nancy Sinatra's "These Boots Are Made for Walkin'."

Apparently I took the matter seriously. When I was nine, I cut a coupon out of *TV Guide* that advertised a school for talented children. I filled it out, walked to the mailbox, and posted it. When I got to Aunt Ducky's house and found her on the phone (with my mother, as it turned out), I leapt to an erroneous conclusion.

"Ducky, don't call an agent for me," I told her. "I have my own."

My older brother, Gordon Thomas Gardner, owned all the albums of the Beatles, the Supremes, Herb Alpert, Janis Joplin, Jimi Hendrix, and numerous rock groups. My love for that music, acquired by the age of ten, remained with me in my heart and in my soul. They influenced my adult career and continue to do so.

I was not strong in math, but I excelled at creative writing. History intrigued me, too, and art. Whenever we made a gift to bring home for Mother's Day or Easter—a clay hand print, a ceramic turtle, découpage, or a wood-burning project—I always had it unwrapped by the time I got it home. I was so eager to show it to my mother that I couldn't keep it hidden very long. It was important to me to please my parents and make them proud of me.

Gordy was eight years older, and I suppose that he viewed me as the bratty little brother. He was always supportive, though. He was a high school football player and a strong student, too. He went on to college at USC, then to Emory University in Atlanta, Georgia, for dental school. Eventually he returned to California to open a practice in Santa Monica.

Like Gordy I played various sports as a child. My father was one of the coaches of the neighborhood Little League team. I played second base, although I didn't like it very much. I'm not sure of the reason. Perhaps it was because, with a December birthday, I was always the youngest in my class. Since I was smaller than the rest of the boys, they tended to pick on me.

I had the good fortune to be a fast runner, however, so I loved relay races and other events involving speed. In elementary school I liked to work out on the gymnastics apparatus, especially the high bar and parallel bars. My father erected a high bar in our backyard to complement the basketball hoop in the front. Since we already had a tetherball pole, he simply put up a second pole and a bar that connected the two. I was able to swing myself around to my heart's content. That built up blisters on my hands that later irritated Tai. She told me that I had "cooties," a widespread imaginary childhood infestation usually possessed by members of the opposite sex.

I was born in Los Angeles on September 22, 1959. My parents couldn't agree on a name, so my Japanese godfather, Mako Nakashima, suggested Tai. He said that it meant *beautiful*. I was given the middle name Reina, Spanish for *queen*.

My family lived in Los Angeles, below Pico Boulevard and east of La Cienega. My street was Sierra Bonita. If you drove north, the next street over was Gardner. Isn't that odd? Maybe my partnership with Randy was just meant to be.

My neighborhood was a melting pot of nationalities and ethnic groups. The population wasn't uniformly white, black, or Hispanic. My mother, Cleo, whose family came from Shreveport, Louisiana, was black. My father, Constancio Sr. (Connie), who died in 1996, was half Filipino and half Hopi Indian. My brother, Constancio Jr., was much darker than I, so each of us was a different color. That mix was perfectly normal in Los Angeles. We didn't give it a thought.

I have always been very accepting of my ethnic background. I don't categorize myself. In all of our years together, my background has never been an issue for Randy—or for anyone else, as far as I know.

With my dad.

My mom, the tennis player.

A lot of cake. Constancio's side was pink. Mine was blue. The bakery mixed up the order because they thought that Tai was a boy's name.

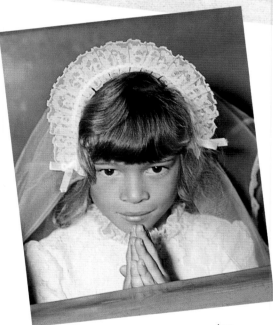

My first communion.

At age six.

At nine months.

One and One Make a Pair

There were numerous children in our neighborhood. We played outside more often than we did indoors. We entertained ourselves with hide-and-go-seek until the sky got dark and our parents called us in.

My family lived in a two-bedroom duplex, so my brother and I shared a room. There was the girlie side, and then there was Constancio's side that overflowed with model cars and posters. He was three years older, but we got along quite well. He watched out for me. I don't remember fighting with him, although he teased me a lot.

Constancio was the natural athlete of the family. He was good at tennis—all of us in the family were tennis players—and football, softball, and virtually anything else that he tried. I believe that he had a hard time being told what to do, though. He disliked the discipline of sports, while I thrived on discipline.

Constancio and I went to a Catholic school, Saint Mary Magdalene at the corner of Pico and La Cienega, until I was in third grade. I actually wanted to be a nun, but I suspect that all the little girls did. The nuns drilled that ambition into us. I don't know what snapped me out of it. Maybe figure skating. The nuns' power intrigued me. Boy, were they strict. They had so many rules.

I loved their look, those powerful ladies in black. I wondered about them while I played on the playground. One by one they went up into their convent. What did they do there? Did they play games? Did they eat? If so, what did nuns eat? Did they take off their wimples at mealtime? What kind of stockings did they wear under those heavy black shoes? It all baffled and fascinated me.

I no longer subscribe to some of the religious beliefs that the nuns and priests taught me during those days, but I still like the formality of Catholicism. As a child I loved wearing the school uniform. It was orderly. Many years later I rebelled. Totally!

Constancio and I had a great childhood. I remember the huge joint birthday parties that my parents threw for us because our birthdays were close together. (His is September 12. Mine is just ten days later.) We always had massive amounts of cake.

I didn't see much of my father. He worked constantly to support us. He was on the LAPD. for twenty-six years, first as a sergeant in the Parker Center jail division that became infamous during the O.J. Simpson case, then as a detective sergeant in Holly-wood. He loved his job, although he didn't talk about it much. He didn't bring it home. Policemen are taught to keep cool, and he did.

Dad was also the head of security at Paramount Studios, and he held a second part-time security job during my costly competitive years. My mother was always a full-time homemaker.

We had rules in our house: no cursing, for example. Our parents required my brother and me to clean our room. For a policeman, though, my father wasn't excessively strict at home.

Randy will tell you that in my father's eyes I could do no wrong. I was Daddy's little girl. Dad was always videotaping and photographing me. He showed his love in that way, although he might not have verbalized his feelings as much as I wanted him to. He and my mother had some communication troubles as well, but they loved one another.

In 1970, the year before the San Fernando (Sylmar) earthquake, our family moved to Mission Hills in the San Fernando Valley. The move was a bit of a culture shock. It seemed to me that all the other people who lived in the Valley were white. We were a different-looking family from those they were used to. Things had been fine in Los Angeles, where interracial couples were common. Once we moved, life became more difficult, especially for my brother.

Kids can be vicious to each other. Some of them called Constancio names—the N word, for example—that we had never heard before. I was exotic looking and lighter-skinned, so when people saw my brother and me together, they didn't quite understand how we could be related. That reaction was confusing to us for the first several years in Mission Hills.

It was good that we went through that trial, my brother and I. Living in the Valley's one-color environment taught us very quickly about life. We learned that not everyone is nice. Not everyone gets it. Not everyone is like our family. Not everyone will love us. That made us tough. It schooled us in human nature.

In other ways I was sheltered. Skating sheltered me, as it does most serious skaters, I think. All we have to do is skate. Our families and coaches do almost everything else for us.

In the Valley my family owned a bigger house than the one we had occupied in the city. I had my own bedroom. *That* was pretty neat. My mom and I decorated it in green gingham checks and white eyelet lace. I collected Holly Hobbie and Betsy Clark items, and I played with Barbie dolls until sixth grade. I liked to pretend.

My Barbie was organized. She had a great house with a very neat closet. However, my brother liked to put me through an annoying little routine. I took pains to set up the house just the way I wanted it, with all of its various furnishings. Then Constancio and his friends came along and knocked it over. That was okay, though, because I loved setting it up all over again. It took me a while to shake the Barbie doll obsession.

During the early years my family had a wonderful, traditional life. We ate dinner together at the same time each night, a custom that has virtually vanished from modern-day America. But it all changed when I started skating seriously. It *all* changed.

I loved the ice shows that my parents took me to as a child. When I was old enough, I began skating on weekends just for fun at the Culver Ice Arena with my neighborhood friends.

The first time I stepped onto the ice remains very clear in my memory. The rink was icy cold. It smelled musty. I recall casting frequent furtive downward glances at those unfamiliar objects on my feet. First I held onto the railing. Before long I gathered my courage and skated away, free of constraints. I wasn't afraid. I remember loving the breeze, feeling the speed, being able to propel myself with the glide. I believe that I showed early promise, and I had a real ambition for skating. One day the rink supervisor gave me a little yellow ticket for speeding on the ice. The fine was two cents. That was when skating was still affordable.

After the first couple of skating sessions my parents set me up with a teacher, Alex Lindgren. Each lesson lasted fifteen or twenty minutes. Alex suggested group classes with Mabel Fairbanks, where we learned all the basics: how to stroke forward and backward, do crossovers, and come to a clean stop without crashing into the boards.

First I wore rental skates. Then my parents bought me a used pair of black boy's skates from the rink's little pro shop. Eventually I got new ones, probably stock boots. After just a few weeks of group lessons, Mabel suggested to my parents that I start private lessons with her, so I did.

I loved skating to music. My first solo program was a *Mary Poppins* number, "A Spoonful of Sugar." When I performed that routine at the rink carnival, I forgot my choreography. I freaked out and just froze for a minute before I picked up and continued. That trauma eventually befalls every skater.

The first time I skated was at a birthday party at the Pickwick Arena in Burbank near Christmastime 1965. I was six, and I had never been to an ice rink. I had never even seen *skates*. My godfather, who liked to figure skate, drove me to Pickwick and deposited me on the ice. I cried when the other party guests went out into the middle of the oval. The rink was full of boisterous children playing crack the whip. I was freezing cold, and I didn't like the smell of the arena. The whole thing just scared me. It was too much. I told my godfather, "I don't like this. Take me home."

Then one day I saw Peggy Fleming on television. I know that it was Peggy. I remember that bouffant hairdo. She looked like a fairy to me. She floated, and she *still* floats. That was when I told myself that I wanted to try skating again.

We lived not too far from the Culver Ice Arena on Sepulveda Boulevard. My mother saw some advertising and took me to try it out. I liked skating better the second time. Having seen it on television, I understood what it was about. After studying Peggy I thought hopefully, "Maybe I can do that."

I had a second ambition as well. I wanted very much to go to art school to learn to be a painter. There was a beautiful building on Wilshire Boulevard near the art museum that housed a prestigious art school with a very good children's class. I was accepted, took one class, and loved it. Afterward my mother told me, "We can't afford both art and skating. You have to pick one."

Since my brother also participated in sports at the time, we truly couldn't support both activities for me. I remember making the decision as I stood there in front of the art class, watching the other children having so much fun with their paints. I was torn for a moment. Then I announced, "I want to skate." I didn't know it then, but I had chosen by far the more expensive pursuit.

My legs were spindly, but we didn't have leg warmers back then. I skated in tights, a dress, a sweater, and gloves, and I was always cold. The art classroom would have been warmer, but for some reason I really loved that chilly, foggy rink. Something kept drawing me back to it. Most of my friends were there, and the environment felt safe. It was the perfect institutional babysitter.

I started lessons with a Canadian teacher, Dan Corbet. First I took a couple of group lessons, then some private ones. A skating judge, Tony Garcia, suggested to my mother, "Tai should try Mabel Fairbanks's group classes."

Randy was a much better skater than I was at the time. He was already taking private lessons from Mabel, and his repertoire included an Axel, the most difficult single jump. The Axel required a forward takeoff and a half-revolution more than any of the other jumps. Some of the children liked to sit on the rail and count out loud how many Axels Randy could perform in a row. *One, two, three* ... His Axels were quick, and his boots had golden blades. I remember watching in fascination as he showed off.

All of us spent our break time more or less together. There was only one warm-up room and a coffee shop where the other girls and I set up my Barbie dolls. Whenever Randy came along, he looked at the dolls, laughed, and pulled their hair.

I remember chatting with Tai about her dolls. She was nearly a year and nine months younger and extremely shy. She had light brown hair that she wore in braids, and she hung out with the other little girls.

Mabel decided to put the two of us together as Dr. and Mrs. Doolittle for the All-Year Figure Skating Club show, and she had to bribe us with candy to get us to cooperate. It's not that we didn't like each other, but we were kids. *Yuck! Skating with a girl*.

The first time, Mabel made us go around the rink holding hands. I don't remember much more than that. We probably skated forward and backward. I couldn't lift Tai much at all, just little baby waist lifts. I certainly couldn't get her over my head. I was ten, and I was a scrawny little kid.

I remember Mabel saying, "Hold hands and stroke around the rink together." She tried us out to see if we matched at all. I don't believe that she discussed the idea with our parents. It was just a notion that popped into her head.

I didn't want to hold Randy's hand. His Axel intimidated me. An Axel was a big thing. I think that Mabel and the older children bribed me with doll clothes and candy. Anything to get Randy and me to skate together. The other kids thought that our efforts were humorous. They laughed behind our backs.

At the dress rehearsal for our first big show, Randy's pants ripped during a split jump—wide open, right in the crotch. The pants were made of green satin. We didn't have much stretch fabric in those days. Randy could perform a perfect split jump, but that day it did him in. The rest of us all giggled. With the pants sewn up in time for the evening performance, the Doolittles were a hit.

Mabel loved having her picture taken with her kids.

One of our baby lifts.

One and One Make a Pair

Two of Mabel's older students were Richard Ewell and Michelle McCladdie, the first pairs team I ever saw. Richard was an amazing skater who competed in both singles and pairs. He eventually became the 1970 U.S. junior men's champion and, with Michelle, the 1972 junior pairs champion. I could watch Peggy Fleming, a singles skater, on television. But it was Richard and Shelley alone who embodied pairs skating for me. Beyond them I didn't have a clue.

Randy and I began by matching our strokes and performing side-by-side spins, spirals, and shoot-the-duck moves. We did a lot of posing. I don't remember being scared at that point. I just didn't really know what I was doing. I went along with the pairs skating only because Mabel told me to. It wasn't fun then. I didn't *know* Randy yet. There was no real communication between us, just a lot of giggling. We both still preferred to skate singles. That was our thing.

We did get attention from the other children, though. That's for sure. They all involved themselves in making Randy and me practice. We became their group project. *Let's get these two kids to skate.* When I was learning a simple press lift on the ice, my friends all got beneath me—that is when the fear started because I was high in the air—and one, two, three, they pushed me up while Randy stood there with his arms shaking. *We're all here for you, Tai. Just do it. Now stay still.*

Oh god, I was scared. I was the baby, everyone's little sister. The teenaged girls in particular adopted me.

When I started private lessons with Mabel, mornings began very early. I had to wake up my parents and get them moving by 5:00 A.M. *Come on. Let's go.* I hated to be late. On the days when my parents or other children's folks couldn't drive us to the rink, Mabel picked us all up at our homes, just like a school bus. I couldn't wait to hear the honk of her horn in front of my house. I was always right at the door, worrying. *I'm going to be late. I'm going to be late.* I lived for the moment when she arrived. I could hear the honk of her horn and a screech of tires as she stopped on a dime.

It was always foggy in the rink. Because we children were little, the fog rose higher than our heads. While we patched—practiced figures—no one could see us. It was like hide-and-go-seek beneath the fog. After we finished our figures, some of us went to school. I often begged for a reprieve. *Mabel, may I please stay out of school? I need to work on my double Salchow.*

I loved school at that age. I just loved skating more. Skating was more interesting to me, and I was making great friends. Because I spent more time at the rink than at school, I felt more connected there. We young skaters were like a family.

Mabel had a unique style, flamboyant for the times. Her hair was red, and she always looked beautiful to me. She made things interesting by wearing different-colored skates on different days: purple, pink, beige, or silver.

Mabel was strict, though. There was no fooling around, no talking. She had a great many students, but she knew where each of us was at any given time. She always knew if we were goofing off. I don't want to say that she gave us spankings, but she applied little taps if she saw that we weren't working. She pulled us over and said, "Don't waste your parents' money. Don't waste my time." She was right. But when it was appropriate, she let us have fun. Those were good times.

Mabel taught us to believe in ourselves. She told all her children, "Suffer for your art." *What? Suffer for my art? What art? I'm skating!* As silly as it sounded to a young child, that idea stuck with me. I still use the phrase in my everyday life.

Mabel motivated us. She instilled confidence in us. *See how that girl jumped? You can jump ten times higher.* Yes, we could, and we did. Randy and I were always the best jumpers at the rink. We always learned the jumps more quickly than anyone else did. Mabel knew what she was doing with respect to technique, but there was more to her success. We connected with her on a personal level.

I had the most fun when I stayed overnight at Mabel's house. She often hosted Friday night sleepovers. Children would fill her house to the rafters. Our favorite entertainment, *Love, American Style*, didn't come on until ten, and it was a big thing for me to stay up and watch it. Mabel was so good to us. She was our second mom, our babysitter. Our parents felt safe leaving us in her care.

One of the things I loved to do was go into Mabel's bedroom and look through her jewelry boxes. There was something frightening in that bedroom, too: a big dresser with a mirror. When I was young, I didn't point my toes enough when I skated. Mabel warned me, "If you don't start pointing your toes, I'm going to cut your feet off and put them in that dresser." From then on I was very attentive to the position of my feet. Mabel had that power.

After we all woke up on Saturday mornings, Mabel took us to the rink. She had a copper-colored Cougar hatchback, and she drove it fast. She also made U-turns and ran red lights. She wasn't a great driver. We stuffed ourselves into that Cougar, three in the front seat and four in the back. I was small, so I lay across the laps in the rear. That was before the government enacted seatbelt laws. We took some wild rides.

Mabel had a key to the back door of the rink. We put our things in lockers and stayed all day long, public session after public session after public session. Saturday was an all-day skate. We loved it. Our only break came at lunchtime when we went to McDonald's or to the dairy store.

Mabel was quite graceful and light on her feet. In addition to skating she taught us ballet, jazz, meditation, and proper breathing. Richard Ewell brought a TV into the ballet room on Saturdays so we could watch Janet Lynn if she happened to be on ABC's *Wide World of Sports*.

In those days Randy and I were just two singles skaters skating side by side, with the occasional lift or spin at each end of the ice. We got together at some point to set up our lift, then went back to skating *here* and *there*. We had a throw Axel, a pull spiral, and a pull-camel spin. Randy just tossed his arm like *this,* and I jumped on my own. That was our throw Axel. I remember Mabel standing at the railing telling us what to do.

When my family moved to the Valley, I enrolled at a public school, but I was so involved in skating that I couldn't concentrate in class. I just wanted to be at the ice

(Jim and Sonia Brown)

(William Udell)

During our Years

with Mabel

(William Udell)

(William Udell)

(William Udell)

rink. My parents should have invested in the 405 freeway. Mom got up at dawn to chauffeur me to the rink, then waited to drive me to school. The traffic wasn't as bad then as it is now. The trip took half an hour each way. I remember sleeping in the back of our station wagon.

The summers were the best times, when we didn't have school to worry about. Other skaters came from around the country to train and compete in Los Angeles. I remember Scott Hamilton as a little hotshot from Bowling Green, Ohio. He was very amusing as a child. In age he was between Randy and me. We first met him in 1970, when he had just turned twelve, at a competition at Culver Ice Arena. There was a freestyle event called Golden West that usually took place at our rink in late summer. That was Scott's first long-distance trip to a competition.

It was so much fun. Scott came out from Ohio as a solo skater, but he also competed in ice dance with a little black girl named Edwaa. They were so cute. Scott was a tiny blond thing. He was in awe of Richard Ewell, who could really jump and do great Russian splits. To him Richard was a god. I remember the day when Scott came in to practice with Randy and me, and Mabel helped him and Edwaa with their program. Scott and Edwaa placed third in bronze free dance, and Scott finished second in pre-bronze freestyle.

We heard from the rumor mill that Scott was little for his age because he had had a serious disease. But he was a talented skater and very polite and outgoing. Everyone

Mabel Fairbanks

Mabel Fairbanks believed that God had put her on earth to integrate figure skating—and she did, virtually single-handedly. As a black New York child of the 1930s, she practiced in Central Park wearing primitive black skates purchased at a pawnshop for a dollar. She clipped some newspaper coupons and talked her way into an indoor rink at an hour when most of the Caucasian skaters had left.

One birthday Mabel received new $5.95 white figure skates from Macy's basement. She begged to be allowed into the rink again. Finally the manager said, "Oh, let her in. She has a pair of new skates. She can't do any damage."

"You can't skate with our kids, nigger," white parents spat. "Get off this ice." But the instructors, charmed by Mabel's natural ability, gave her free lessons.

Although she was skilled enough, Mabel knew that she would never skate competitively. Skating clubs didn't admit colored children. She set her sights on a professional career but learned that the shows didn't want her either. That was when she acquired a manager who built her a six-foot-by-six-foot ice rink that she kept, fully functional, in her bedroom. She filled the wood-and-tin structure with dry ice and water and practiced all day long. Sometimes she even slept in

her skates. She hauled the makeshift rink to paid exhibitions.

As a teacher, Mabel fought to gain black children entrance to rinks, helped them become individual members of the USFSA (and eventually of private clubs), gave them free lessons, built their confidence, and served as their advocate in the highly-charged political arena of skating.

"I can't be the only one out there," she declared. "God didn't intend it that way. He put me into teaching to integrate this thing."

Stricken with myasthenia gravis, Mabel continued to sit rinkside, offering free help to anyone who asked, virtually until her death in September 2001.

Tai and Randy took individual lessons for a couple of years, and they were very, very good. Fast learners. When it was time for the club's show, each pro was allowed so many numbers for his or her students. I had space for only one more: either Tai or Randy. "Well," I thought, "if the club only wants one more number, then Tai and Randy will do that one number together." I paired them up, and they got a standing ovation.

Later I told them, "Hey, kids, if you are that good in so short a time, why don't we go in for competitions?"

loved him. In the early days, though, he didn't take his skating very seriously. When he missed something, he joked about it.

Nowadays he pursues his skating career with a vengeance. As Randy puts it, he goes cuckoo over it. I don't know what drives him. He has been known to say, "What else am I going to do but skate?" The fact is that he has everything in the world going for him.

After Golden West we didn't run into Scott for a number of years—not until he moved to Colorado to train with Carlo Fassi. Then we saw him regularly at the summer shows in Denver. When the flirty, little-girl stuff started for me, I developed a crush on Scott. (He admitted later that the interest had been mutual.) But then I had a crush on everyone—Peter Oppegard, Peter Carruthers, all the cute boys.

The first USFSA competition that Randy and I entered as a pair was the 1971 Southwest Pacific Regionals, novice division, at our home rink. I wore a dress, and Randy wore his little jumpsuit. The outfits were black with big V-necks. I had always worn my mother's home-sewn two-piece outfits with separate trunks, so it was a big thing for me to have a one-piece dress. We skated to "Baby Face" and finished sixth in a field of ten. Randy did well in the intermediate men's event and qualified for the Pacific Coast Sectionals that year.

At that competition I wore my first pair of Harlick boots. They had belonged to Gina

They said no. I said, "Yes, let's try it."

"I don't want to hold his hand."

"I don't want to hold *her* hand either, so we won't skate together."

"You are going to do it anyway because you will be sensational. In 1976 you will be on the Olympic team. At the following Olympics you will win."

Everybody laughed at me, but I always judged by children's heads. I looked at Tai and Randy's heads and said, "Those kids are going to be great skaters."

Some of the parents wondered, "How can she tell by their *heads* what they are going to do?"

I explained, "There are brains up there, and they will do it. Please believe me. They will be fantastic."

I had a big house at the foot of the Hollywood Hills on a dead end street that went up into the mountains. The children always called it the haunted house. I am telling you, those kids would come over, and we would have a ball. I had a big backyard where we made barbecue, and the children had the run of the house.

Tai and Randy were really dedicated. They were such wonderful children. I always told my students, "Every time you get on this ice to practice, you suffer for your art. Then, at competition time, you go out and enjoy yourself. You earned it. That championship belongs to you."

I loved to see my students jump over the moon. *Just get up there and go—as far as your mind will let you.* I had high jumpers.

Tai and Randy won little novice championships here and there. From Regionals, we went to Sectionals. Then one day I said to them, "Look, I'm not getting along too well with the club here. I want my students to join the Los Angeles Figure Skating Club." They did, and they continued to do well. Then one day their parents decided to send them over to the Santa Monica ice skating rink on Fifth Street near the ocean to work with John Nicks.

Tai and Randy would have won the Olympics if Randy hadn't had that ailment. I know it. I watched them on TV and just cried and cried and cried. It was so sad, knowing that they would have won.

When I was inducted into the USFSA Hall of Fame in 1997, we had such a wonderful time. Tai gave me the clothes that I wore. If I had anything special to do, she always bought my outfit. She just seemed to know what to buy. Tai and Randy have always been true blue.

Martin, the daughter of singer and actor Dean Martin. Gina never used her equipment much before she took a break from skating. The sport was only an occasional hobby for her, so she wore boots a few times before outgrowing them. Although Gina was a bit older than I was, I had big feet. I inherited all her skates. That hand-me-down system worked perfectly for me.

Eventually, I think, Randy's and my parents must have realized that Mabel had given us all that she could. We were still in the novice ranks and hadn't really gone anywhere: second at Regionals, then third at the December 1971 Pacific Coast Sectionals.

Maybe that was a clue to them that it was time for us to move on. Maybe we weren't excelling in the way that they hoped we would or thought we should. Perhaps somebody in the skating hierarchy had spoken to them about our lack of substantial progress.

Whatever their reasons, our parents talked to John Nicks and made up their minds to move us to him. It was really their decision, not ours. Randy and I always followed the path that the adults in our lives charted. Switching to Mr. Nicks was a big turning point for us. I was twelve then, and Randy was fourteen.

Over the years Mabel watched us on television when we competed. Whenever we next saw her, she would have her list of things that she thought needed work. I always listened. Mabel knew when I wasn't giving enough—or when I wasn't pointing my toes. She still knew.

(William Udell)

That's Linda Fratianne with me in the early 1970s in a Los Angeles FSC show at the Pickwick Rink. The boys are Scott Carson and Paul Cooney. (William Udell)

At Yosemite with Constancio. My dad called this picture "Jump."

chapter three

The Nicks Years

Mabel had taken us from the lowliest local events up to novice pairs at the sectional level, but it was John Nicks who coached all the top senior teams. He had just moved from Paramount Iceland to the new Ice Capades Chalet on Broadway Street in Santa Monica. We knew him by reputation. He had Olympic-caliber skaters in his camp.

Our parents effected the transition to Mr. Nicks right after Pacific Coasts at the end of 1971. Mabel was fine with the situation. She understood. For us to rise in the standings and get the training that we needed, it would be both an honor and a benefit

John Nicks with his sister Jennifer.

to work with someone like John Nicks.

John Nicks! That was exciting. He was *the* coach. He brought his champions with him to Santa Monica. I remember his first orientation meeting with Randy and me and our parents. During the long walk to his office at the back of the rink, I felt scared. *Oh my gosh, this man is so powerful, so intimidating—and he doesn't say much.*

Mr. Nicks informed us that he was going to take us on, and *this* was what was going to happen. Randy and I were still skating as singles in addition to pairs, so the schedule Mr. Nicks worked out for us was crazy. There were rules, guidelines, admonitions, and statements. *This* is how you are going to wear your hair. As it happened, I already wore my hair the way Mr. Nicks wanted it, but I certainly would have changed the style to suit him if that had been necessary.

Randy was a little scared of Mr. Nicks, too. And we always called him *Mr. Nicks*. We still do. He oversaw a strict, intense training atmosphere. It was serious stuff. He required his students to keep up the standards of skating technique and of personal behavior.

He taught us a lot about class and manners. He even showed us how to pose on the podium. His instruction was detailed. There was a right way to get on the ice. There was a right way to get off. If you had a problem with your performance, you took it outside. No matter how horribly you skated, you smiled. You didn't roll your eyes. You didn't pace with your hands on your hips. You didn't read the judges' marks and groan, "God, look at that. She gave me a 5.1." Mr. Nicks would have nailed us—and if he hadn't, my mother would have.

That was why Mr. Nicks was a great overall coach. He prepped us for many things as we got older and entered the limelight. He molded us as athletes and competitors, organized our career, and taught us the fine points. He expected us always to be on time. We couldn't goof around during training sessions. He held little impromptu competitions, especially during the summer, lining up all his students along the rail and making us skate out and do jumps. We didn't want to miss in front of our peers.

When we joined Mr. Nicks at the end of 1971, JoJo Starbuck and Ken Shelley, three-time U.S. champions and our heroes, were about to leave for the Sapporo Olympics. We watched and watched as they ran through their programs. Kenny was the one I particularly studied. He had to practice his figures, his two singles programs, and his pairs material. There was no monkey business.

John Nicks

If Tai and Randy were intimidated, they can blame my British training. I learned in the first three or four years of coaching that I could not coach in the United States the same way as they coach in England—and that is to the benefit of the United States! In England, at least in the years that I was there, it tended to be a little bit more formal. Basically the coach had the final authority and responsibility in the ice rink and wasn't involved too much with the students outside the rink. That is not quite so in this country.

Every coach has his own style. I was never Tai and Randy's friend. They had a lot of friends. I was never a father to them. They had their own fathers. I was their coach, and that was the relationship I had with them. It was a relationship, I think, of mutual respect.

When we found out that JoJo and Kenny went to Al and Harriet De Ray's dance school, Tai and I began doing the same thing. We studied ballet with Harriet. Al taught us lifts on the floor, helped us with strength training, and did some gymnastics with us: back bends, handstands, and that kind of thing. Our work with the De Rays was our first off-ice training. The air was always hot in that little studio, but the effort paid off.

After JoJo and Kenny graduated from the amateur ranks and joined Ice Capades, Mr. Nicks still had some senior teams, but I knew that the focus was on us at that point, even though we were just entering the junior division. We were his future as a coach. At the same time he taught some of our competitors.

Our new training regime, on and off the ice, occupied our minds and fired our imaginations as nothing else could—including traditional education.

Randy and I went to the same school during our first year with Mr. Nicks: Culver City Junior High. After our 6:30 A.M. patch session Randy's father drove us to school. The administration allowed us to arrive at 9:15 and excused us from physical education. We didn't see much of each other in school, but if I walked past Randy's locker just as he was about to put away an armload of books, for some reason I thought that it was funny to kick the locker shut.

My mother picked us up at about 2:30 P.M. and returned us to the rink. The other students shot me questioning looks. *Why does she get to leave early?*

Randy and I always sat in the back of my mother's station wagon and entertained ourselves by making fun of other people or each other. I sat with my skate bag in the cargo area while Randy read in the second seat. I liked to tell him, "Don't look now!" When he turned around anyhow, my skate blade would be right in his face.

When we arrived at the rink after school, we skated the public session. Then we did a patch and a freestyle session. We got Saturdays off to go to our dance class with the De Rays in Hollywood. Then we skated again on Sunday morning.

I completed seventh grade, though I often fell asleep in class. My marks weren't great. I didn't like math, and it showed. I just couldn't keep up with the work after getting up so early in the morning to skate. Randy handled the demands better than I did.

Before and after school were the times when I had fun. I felt very isolated in junior high. I felt *different*. My heart was in skating. School was a distraction. I never sensed that I was missing out on things like dances and after-school activities. There were no regrets, then or now. I simply wasn't interested. The events of my subsequent life have more than made up for anything that I may have missed then. You can't have everything. If you excel at one endeavor, that is enough—although a skater does need to maintain some outside interests in order to achieve a balance, to have outlets, and to keep the skating fresh.

At the Pickwick club show.

Practicing at the Santa Monica Ice Capades Chalet.

Trying a swan lift for Al De Ray, it was hard to find the balance point.

Harriet De Ray, our first ballet teacher.

Look at that pose! (William Udell)

Arctic Blades, our first competition with Mr. Nicks.

Backstage at Ice Capades with JoJo.

Tai as a flower caddy at the 1972 Nationals at Long Beach. (William Udell)

The Nicks Years

I spent a lot of off-ice time with my rink friends. The rink was only about four blocks from the ocean, which was great. We could walk to the beach after skating. The Canadians who came down to train seemed to spend more time at the beach than they did at the rink. They were a little older than the rest of us, so Mr. Nicks rented them a beach house. The Canadian contingent always had the best tans and the prettiest girls.

Allen Schramm was a men's competitor from the central Bay Area of Northern California who sometimes came down to Los Angeles to train. Allen was a great skater, unusual and wild. He was fun to be around. I always liked it when he came to town. Perry Jewell, another men's competitor, came in from Phoenix and eventually moved here. David Kirby was another of my rink buddies.

Tai's skating friends were Marina Drasnin, Shelley Palmer, Linda Fratianne, Carrie Rugh, and Lisa-Marie Allen: "a little pack of wild girls," Tai calls them. Marina was her best friend. Always the artist, better at painting than at skating, she didn't love to compete the way Tai and I did. Tai and Marina are still like sisters.

Robert Wagenhoffer was around during those days, too. I loved Robert. He was one of the best, blessed with so much natural talent. I was jealous of him. He was one of those guys who didn't have to train hard. He just went out on the ice and did whatever he

Junior pairs at Pacific Coasts. Those camel spins are pretty well matched!

wanted to. He had it all: great spring, jumps, spins, artistry, line.

The year Tai and I went to our first Worlds, Robert and his pairs partner, Vicki Heasley, went with us. Eventually Robert left pairs skating to concentrate on singles, then quit while he was one of the top three men in the country. His figures weren't great, and I guess that he realized that the judges weren't going to give him the national title with Scott Hamilton around. Besides, Robert was at an age by then when he was emotionally ready to move on and turn professional.

Looking back now, I do wonder what it would have been like to go to the prom or to watch a high school football game. At the time, though, I could not have cared less. I didn't think about dating. I dreamed about my next costume and my new music. Those were the important things on my mind.

In the middle of eighth grade I quit Culver City Junior High School and acquired a tutor from Valley Professional School, Marge Van Valkenburg. Soon we all went to Marge, including Randy. Her clientele consisted of actors, dancers, and skaters. Either we went to her house or she came to ours. I don't remember learning much, especially when she tutored us at the rink. That was torture.

The State of California required something like four hours of schoolwork a day. We learned the same material that our public school teachers would have taught us. The atmosphere simply wasn't as intense.

Marge had a daughter who skated, so she understood what we were going through. I did the necessary work and eventually received a diploma from Colin McEwen High School in Malibu, even though schoolwork still seemed liked a distraction. I much preferred learning on the ice. There everything was new. Randy and I were improving as a pair. It was exciting to be part of a serious training structure.

Mr. Nicks used key words and terse phrases. He wasn't chatty. That was hard to get used to after Mabel. Generally he just *looked* at us, and we knew what he wanted us to do.

He didn't like us popping jumps. That made him turn bright red. He didn't approve of us stopping in the middle of a routine. It was better to attempt an element and fall. *Don't stop in the middle of your program. You might as well go home.* If anyone did stop, he turned off the music. We had 78-rpm records then instead of tapes, and I saw a few records fly across the rink. Not ours. Randy and I learned to push through our programs. We didn't want our records flying across the rink in front of our friends and all the other coaches.

If Mr. Nicks walked off your lesson and retreated to his office, that was not fun. He had a one-way window that he could look through, but we couldn't see in. I didn't like that. The worst thing was to be told to leave the ice because you weren't trying. Mr. Nicks did not like to see someone refuse to give it his all.

Randy and I were hard-working kids. We knew that skating was business for us. We began to do well in competitions, and the sport became more expensive. Our parents made remarks that let us know where we stood. *Get serious about this because it is not cheap. Your dad is working three jobs.* Money became an issue.

Our parents worked very hard to get us what we needed. Even that many years ago a pair of skates cost two hundred to two hundred and fifty dollars. Tai and I never went without. We never had to scrounge around for money for food or hotel rooms. In that respect we were very lucky. A lot of skaters did have to scrounge. However, if someone brought up the subject of finances, I would suddenly have to run off and practice my double Axel. Where the money came from was the last thing on my mind when I was young.

Although Tai and I thought and planned only one season at a time, we felt a lot of pressure to work hard. We wanted Mr. Nicks to be proud of us. We didn't want to ruin his great track record. His students were always first. We told ourselves, "Let's be first, too." He was known for making champions. He churned them out, one by one. But he refused to keep a student who wasn't willing to work. He would rather send that student to another coach.

No matter how talented that student was. There were other students who were ten times more talented than I was, in my opinion, but they didn't have the necessary drive. Mr. Nicks instilled that drive—as Mabel did. Some kids gave up or kicked the ice. We didn't do that. We knew better.

We had fun on the days when Mr. Nicks wasn't at the rink. We loved it when he left to attend a competition with other students. But then we felt as though his fellow coaches were spying on us for him.

As a result of our concentrated work, Randy and I learned a lot in a short time. Mr. Nicks trained us quickly. Within little over a year of beginning lessons with him, we won Southwest Sectionals, Pacific Coast Regionals, and the 1973 Junior Nationals in Bloomington, Minnesota. That was when everything started in earnest.

In Bloomington, I finished second in the novice men's event. Scott Hamilton was ninth. I remember coming home and telling myself, "Wow, I'm the national junior pairs champion. People are talking about me."

During the middle grades, I took some minor ribbing for practicing a "sissy" sport. By the time I reached high school age, my friends thought that I was cool, partly because Tai and I were winning titles and partly because we had begun traveling to international competitions.

Tai was always losing things when we traveled: her boarding pass, her room key. She was good at keeping track of the important things, though. Our first trip was to Oberstdorf, West Germany, and St. Gervais, France, for a pair of junior development competitions. Mr. Nicks didn't go with us, but we had team coaches and team leaders, Charles and Elaine DeMore, to watch over us. Barbara Roles, coach of American men's competitor John Carlow, kept an eye on us, too.

1973 Nationals at Bloomington, Minnesota: Junior Champions!

At our hotel.

Going for the junior title.

Notice the big smiles.

Cleo Babilonia and Jan and Jack Gardner.

Those competitions were lots of fun. I had a crush on Charlie Tickner—like everyone else. Even the mothers had crushes on Charlie. He had that curly hair, just like a puppy dog, and he was such a good skater. He made us all melt. We didn't see him often while he trained in the Bay Area, but he was kind and had an appealing, dry sense of humor. Randy and I supported him, and he supported us.

St. Gervais was where Randy and I met Robin Cousins. The Grand Prix was his first international competition, too. We became great friends. I was a fan of his. I loved the fact that he was an artist as well as a skater. I was envious of that. *And you can paint? How dare you?* He always designed his own costumes. He always chose his own music. Robin was self-sufficient at a young age.

Although Randy and I won the Nebelhorn Trophy in Oberstdorf, we suffered a minor disappointment at the St. Gervais Grand Prix. Swiss skaters Karin and Christian Künzle finished first, which was fine with us. The announcer called us out as the silver medalists. We stood on the second step of the podium to receive our little trophies and have our pictures taken. When the ceremony ended, the referee told us, "We made a mistake. You really finished third." We had to trade medals and trophies with the West German team, Corinna Halke and Eberhard Rausch.

After Oberstdorf and St. Gervais the USFSA sent us to Moscow. That was a big thing. We were the first American amateur pair ever to compete there, and I was only thirteen years old. Because Randy and I were the junior national champions, the trip to Russia was the Association's way of seasoning us, getting us ready for our upcoming senior year.

Going to the Soviet Union then was much different from going to Russia now. It was freezing cold, and the Russian people were cold, too. My mother went with us as a chaperon, and I remember asking her, "Why doesn't anyone smile? Why are they all wearing gray and black?"

I always felt as though I was being watched. *Is there a bug or a camera in this room?* I never felt alone.

I wouldn't eat the local food. The Russians had a different way of cooking from what I was used to. My mother, for some reason, had had the foresight to pack foods like tuna and crackers. We all lived on her supplies.

When we got off our New York to Moscow Aeroflot flight, I immediately noticed three things: the cold, the smells, and the fur hats. You could tell that the Russians didn't have much in the way of consumer goods. Even in the better restaurants the meat was unidentifiable. We went with a translator, Rita, to see the Kremlin and other major sights.

I was overwhelmed by our fellow pairs competitors. Tai and I were so young then, and the others were so skillful. There were seven Russian pairs teams—and then us. That was the order of finish, too.

There must have been something special in their strength training. Some of the Soviet skaters did admit to taking steroid shots for muscle development. They knew when to take them and when to stop. The tests to detect banned substances weren't as sophisticated then as they are now.

I never knew of an American skater who was encouraged to take steroids. Tai and I certainly weren't. I didn't even know where to get them—or even what they were, really.

The Canadian skaters at the Moscow competition were friendly to us, so we stuck with them. We were the babies. People considered us "cute." They fussed over us.

In late 1973 everything started to change because of the exposure international competition gave us. Once we participated in televised competitions, people in our neighborhoods treated us differently. The fawning, artificial attention made us a little cynical. I get that still in daily life. If store clerks don't know who I am, they treat me fairly, no more and no less. When I hand them my credit card or write a personal check, suddenly their demeanor changes.

Things began to change at home at the same time. We remained happy, but things were just *different*. The family came apart a bit. We separated. My father couldn't attend my practices or all of my competitions. It was usually my mother who did that. Her activities centered on me. There is just something about skating. I don't know what it is. It consumes an entire family. It can tear you apart if you are not strong.

Ken Shelley

When JoJo and I were first in Ice Capades, John Nicks still choreographed our routines. We went back to Santa Monica in the summer. At the time, Mr. Nicks had quite a few pairs. We all practiced together, and that is my earliest recollection of Tai and Randy.

They were great kids and very hardworking. They were both tiny and thin, and Tai had the skinniest little legs. I thought, "How can this girl even skate?" But you could see that they both had a real passion for skating from the beginning. That is the mark of true champions. Tai and Randy were always happy about being at the rink. They also enjoyed skating *together*. You could see that from the start. Randy was the more outgoing of the two. When I think of Tai, I remember her giggling.

John Nicks was very much in charge of our training. He had a strong presence. He made the decisions. He was a disciplinarian. I do think that he adopted a different manner with Tai and Randy as time went on. Maybe they didn't see it, but from my perspective he mellowed. Even so he was frightening at times, and he had that persona with parents, too. Everyone was on guard.

Mr. Nicks was unemotional, and he expected the same from his skaters. He talked to us about how we presented ourselves when we competed, both in and out of the rink. He was a stickler about showing absolutely no emotion one way or another. If we wanted to be joyous, if we wanted to cry, he expected us to go elsewhere. That was ingrained in our young psyches. It has served me well in certain situations. Because we spent our formative years with him, Mr. Nicks had a profound influence on our lives. He was a wonderful coach, trainer, and teacher.

Like JoJo and I, Tai and Randy also worked a lot with dancer Terry Rudolph. She had staged and directed a dinner theater ice show at the Casa Carioca on the army base in Garmisch, West Germany. When that closed, she came to Southern California and worked with skaters at the Ice Capades Chalets in North Hollywood and Santa Monica, on and off the ice. She had a lot to do with Tai and Randy's success. She "finished" them. Mr. Nicks was good at that, too, but Terry took it to the next level. Tai and Randy became beautiful skaters. Their unison was probably the best of any American pairs team I have seen.

At St.Gervais, Our First International

(Jean Burnier)

(Jean Burnier)

The U.S. team: Jane Pankey, Richard Horne, Kath Malmberg, Linda Fratianne, us, John Carlow, and Charlie Tickner. (Jean Burnier)

My brother was suddenly relegated to the background. He resented that, and he lashed out in various ways. Putting a lock on his bedroom door was one of them. We never knew what he was doing. There could have been a girl in there. (Well, *I* knew. I had my ear against his door, and there *was* a girl in there.) Constancio wasn't neglected. My parents went to his games and matches. Skating was just more consuming—of both time and money.

The photos that I'm finding now are reassuring proof that the Babilonias *were* a family. We *did* have fun. We *did* go on vacations. I cherish the snapshots of the Grand Canyon, Las Vegas, Lake Tahoe, and all the other places we could drive to in our station wagon. During those trips we had very happy times. Once, when we went to Yosemite, my dad took a picture of Constancio and me. Dad loved that picture. He called it "Jump." *Tell your sister to jump; then you'll get all the attention.*

I was the focus of my family, too, because skating was so intense. My brother, being so much older than I, never suffered because of it—as far as I know. At least he never complained. Gordy went to almost all of our national and world championships and to the Olympics. He was proud of me and furnished a great support system. He loved the sport and got to know a lot of the people involved in it, fans as well as skaters. He made many valuable lifelong friendships.

When Gordy attended dental school, we went to visit. My parents saw him more often than I did, because sometimes I had to stay at home to skate. But we all went to Atlanta for his graduation.

Both of my parents attended most of my skating competitions. Depending on their work schedules, sometimes one traveled with me and the other joined us later in the week.

Skating did take its toll on my mother, however, as it takes a toll on a great many skating parents who are suddenly plunged into a system and into a lifestyle that isn't natural to them and that they can't control. The stresses of the skating environment (whether competition stresses, pressure from the USFSA, or the expectations of other parents) aggravated her insecurity. She was caught up in something that she couldn't

Poem by Tai

empty space (for my brother)

much attention centered around me
    in the beginning you never understood
a desire to trade places so many times
    know i never could
times when i doubted your love
    a guilt i can't erase
the lost closeness reappeared
    to fill that empty space

Los Angeles
10/1/84, 9 A.M.

fight. My mom was not known as a risktaker. She would never have told the USFSA, for example, "Either pay for Randy's flight or he is not doing that competition." That would have been too risky.

Mom and Tai didn't always hit it off. Mom's reaction was typically "Blame anything or anybody but Randy." She was very protective of me, so Tai and Cleo sometimes bore the brunt of her frustration. Now that I am older, I see that. I understand it. My mother is not that way anymore. Her reactions then were due to insecurity, the fear of taking a stand, and a reluctance to take risks. She went with the flow, whether or not she liked the flow's direction.

For all the intensity of skating, my parents didn't push me. Tai's parents never pushed her either. Not at all. If Tai's mother saw her playing around at the rink, she would get on her, as any parent would. And she had every right to do so. *Get to work!* However, Tai skated because she wanted to. If she and I had wanted to quit, we could have, but we loved skating.

At Moscow Skate in December 1973.

Part of its attraction was the continuity and certainty of our partnership—even though, in the early days, I didn't feel a real closeness to Tai. We were skating partners, and she was one of my ice rink friends. The majority of my friends, however, were guys my age, while Tai hung out with the younger girls.

Over the years we began to create our own secret language. I don't think that we were conscious of it at the time, but a certain look in her eye or mine, a certain gesture, or a tilt of the head conveyed technical skating data as well as information about our feelings.

Now I can read Tai like a book. I know her various frames of mind. I can tell if she is faking cheerfulness, if she is satisfied, and if she is content. That came about through living parallel lives together over time. It happened so gradually and naturally that I hardly noticed.

There were experiences off the ice that we shared as well. Tai and I continued our study of ballet with a new teacher, Terry Rudolph, who came to the dance studio at the rink several times a week. That was more convenient than going to the De Rays.

I also attended a separate jazz school, where I studied with Roland Dupree and Joe Tremaine. Then I won a scholarship to a big dance academy, the Stanley Holden Dance Center. Mr. Holden taught jazz and tap classes at the Los Angeles Music Center of Performing Arts for Children at the Dorothy Chandler Pavilion. I excelled at jazz, and I loved tap, too. (I still have my tap shoes, and they fit!) My two greatest strengths were agility and versatility in character work.

In the 1970s there was lots of dancing in movies and on television specials and variety shows. *The Flip Wilson Show, The Donny & Marie Show* and others like them regularly employed dancers. Music videos were just coming onto the scene, too. Had I not succeeded at skating, I probably would have done all that, then ended up in New York

JoJo Starbuck

When John Nicks and his sister Jennifer won their world title in 1953, pairs didn't do the elements that Kenny and I needed to win our United States title and be contenders internationally. We went to our first Nationals in 1966. We were third in junior pairs, but that was primarily because of the wonderful John Nicks unison, style, discipline, and good training. We did singles skating and shadow skating with our pairs moves. Because of our similarity in height, things looked very polished, but we didn't have the lifts and certain additional pairs elements that we needed.

My mom thought that it would be helpful if we could find an acrobatics teacher who could spend time helping us learn the lifts on the floor. She found an amazing couple in Hollywood who really impacted our skating: Al and Harriet De Ray. Harriet was a wonderful ballet teacher. She gave us an incredible foundation for everything we did.

Al watched videos of the Russians, and we tried to figure out their lifts. He even built a springboard for us to start on. From that springboard and the floor of his studio, we slowly learned the new elements and brought them to the ice. We often did them wrong. We figured out everything the long, hard way. But Al was a real personality-plus teacher who gave us a lot of enthusiasm and helped us make the most of every move we made. Tai and Randy wisely took that lead and went to Al and Harriet, too. I am so glad that my mother found the De Rays in the Yellow Pages.

In the thirteen years that Kenny and I were with Mr. Nicks as amateurs, we all grew a lot, technically and in every other way. The fascinating thing for Kenny and me was to watch how Mr. Nicks could teach Tai and Randy in about a year everything that it had taken us thirteen years to figure out. Every coach in every generation learns as he teaches, because the sport

City as a dancer on the stage. I even took some singing lessons to broaden my talent base, but my voice wasn't that great, in my opinion.

During our years as senior competitors Tai and I began our day at the rink at 8:15 or 9:00 A.M. with several freestyle sessions. Sometime during the morning we did our hour of ballet with Terry. She was a nice woman but strict. With her you couldn't get away with anything. She had danced professionally in the 1930s and 1940s when all entertainers' repertoires included tap, ballet, jazz, and gymnastics. She taught us back bends, character work, the ballet barre, pointed feet, clean lines, fluidity, and a lot more. I still use her floor warm-ups.

Two or three times a week we went to Bob Anderson, our gymnastics coach, for lifts and off-ice training similar to what they call circuit training today: lifting, jogging, working out on equipment. It was difficult for both of us.

Tai worked hard. She was lean and muscular with strong legs and arms. She was very limber. She had good spring. What really made her an excellent partner, though, was her personality. She was compatible and easygoing, not rebellious. She was receptive to coaching and learned a great deal quickly. In spite of what she says to the contrary, she was very talented, too, as well as graceful and balletic.

My strengths as a skater, I believe, were line, control, good technique, and good spins. I was limber. I could do spirals and spreadeagles, things that many other guys couldn't do, which made our pair more interesting.

Tai and I were similar in height, just over three inches apart when we stopped growing at 5' 5" and 5' 8½". As a result we were forced to create our own style. We couldn't risk doing those high triple twists that Irina Rodnina was known for. We learned them, but we didn't use them in competition. We performed double twists, a big throw double Axel, and side-by-side double Axels and triple Salchows. Tai was a gifted jumper.

constantly evolves. Nothing stays the same. It was exciting to see Tai and Randy grow under John Nicks's tutelage, follow in our footsteps to some degree, and then supersede what we had done. It's like the game of add-on.

Eventually Mr. Nicks would teach all of our moves, and then Tai and Randy's moves, to Kristi Yamaguchi and Rudy Galindo, to Natasha Kuchiki and Todd Sand, and then to Todd with his new partner and now wife, Jenni Meno. It was fascinating to follow that evolution. Once the height difference came into play, usually the repertoire changed accordingly, but Kristi and Rudy did a lot of the things that Kenny and I had originally learned with Mr. Nicks.

Because Tai and Randy and Kenny and I had similar repertoires and styles, and because we were uniquely the same size—all four of us—we did a number together to an electronic, jazzed-up variation of "I'm Always Chasing Rainbows" with classical, fully-orchestrated segments. We did solo and pairs elements with our own partners, but we also switched partners during the number and did death spirals and other moves with each other's partners. We had a move we called the "sandwich" with all four of us very close together.

We performed that number at the Los Angeles Sports Arena for a television special and again at Madison Square Garden for a Superskates event. We wore plain black-and-white costumes. When the camera was on a long shot, you couldn't tell who was who. We all got a huge kick out of doing that number, and we laughed a great deal during the rehearsal process, making fun of ourselves, each other, and of course Mr. Nicks.

But we also created that other dimension, the unison and symmetry, with side-by-side flying camels, spreadeagles, and spirals—moves that other teams weren't doing. Those were what set us apart. Terry and Mr. Nicks were both sticklers for unison. Tai and I worked with mirrors and video. To get the timing exactly right, we repeated our moves over and over.

Lifts were the hardest for me at first. I had to do a lot of weight training to build up my strength. I liked to lift, though. I suppose that, being a guy, I felt that it was my job. Lifts are beautiful. I love watching others do them.

Death spirals took us a long time to develop. We spent at least a year perfecting our back outside death spiral. We worked hard on our line and on the refinement of the edge moves because those were our signatures.

We also worked to develop speed. We had to be fast because Rodnina and her partners were *so* fast. I don't know how they did it.

Since those days of power and elegance, I believe that pairs in general have gone too far. Rather than learning to do correct back outside death spirals, for example, contemporary teams go for the glitz by cramming as many improbable positions as they can into their lifts. Most pairs today aren't as versatile as in the past. Granted they are learning harder tricks, but then they aren't consistently accomplishing those tricks. I would rather see less done better.

Tai and I relied on John Nicks to select our music. It was classical for the most part in those days. We trusted his judgment. He played something for us and asked us if we liked it. Usually we did. Sometimes our parents made suggestions as well.

We stepped onto the senior ladder quickly and moved at a steady pace. We made our first World Team in 1974, the year when I won the national junior men's championship in Providence, Rhode Island. Johnny Johns and Melissa Militano became the U.S. senior pairs champions for the second time that year. Tai and I just wanted to be on the team with them. We finished second at Nationals, then tenth at the world championships, where we were the youngest pair ever to represent the United States at Worlds.

Tai and I walked around Munich, Germany, with our mouths open. I remember watching in fascination as Irina Rodnina warmed up backstage by jumping rope. We were interested in observing a variety of training techniques, on and off the ice.

Six-time Canadian champion Toller Cranston gave the best performance of his life, in my opinion, at the Munich exhibitions. He performed the piece that became his signature, *Pagliacci*, and he was brilliant! He had one of those out-of-body experiences that we all have once or twice in our careers. The audience stood and screamed. Oh my God, the costume! The hair! It was all so different and magical.

Toller was a bit older than we were, and he was at his peak in 1974. Although his persona was intimidating to us as teenagers, he was nice to us, both then and later.

The 1974 Nationals at Providence, Rhode Island

Becoming the youngest-ever U.S. World Team pair.

On the podium with Ben Wright, Melissa Militano, Johnny Johns, Erica Susman, and Thomas Huff.

Toller sold his art prints at the arena. I have one of his early pieces, *Sacred Guilt*. He signed it to me. Meeting Toller was a highlight of Munich. He told us, "You guys are going to make it." That was like a blessing from the Pope.

Munich was the place where I first witnessed true drama on the ice. The U.S. champion, Dorothy Hamill, skated after the West German woman, Gerti Schanderl, in Gerti's hometown. The crowd booed Gerti's low marks, and Dorothy, imagining that they were booing her, left the ice in tears. Her coach, Carlo Fassi, and the American team leaders quickly surrounded Dorothy. Her dad also arrived to offer support. She sat down for a while. Then she went out and warmed up again, spun a little in her corner, and cried some more. I had never seen anything like it. When Dorothy finally went out onto the ice to compete, she skated beautifully and won the silver medal.

Some further drama was provoked by our teammate Terry Kubicka's back flip, a move of questionable legality. The judges didn't know what to think about it, but the crowd went nuts.

Just being in the presence of Terry Kubicka, Gordy McKellen, Johnny Johns, Melissa Militano, John Curry, Toller Cranston, and Irina Rodnina was amazing and energizing.

The 1974 Munich Worlds, our first. We were in awe of the other skaters.

A photographer for a German periodical staged this photo in Munich. (Werner Deisenroth)

A publicity shot for Skating *magazine. (J. Keith Williams)*

The next skating season, 1974–75, was a strange one for Randy and me. That was the year when my body changed. I had a growth spurt. I developed a new center of gravity. Everything was off on my end of the team, especially the timing, and I couldn't do anything to improve the situation. *Is she going to keep growing? Is this ever going to end? What will happen?*

One day while we were training a lift, Randy did a half-turn, caught his edge in the ice, and tripped. He somehow tilted me in the air. I fell, and Randy wasn't there to catch me. I landed face first with considerable impact.

I remember a friend shouting, "Here's a tooth!" It had fallen onto the ice. My braces held several other loose teeth in place. If my mouth hurt, I was too stunned to notice. I didn't look to see if there was blood on the ice. The incident happened too quickly.

Someone called an ambulance. The medics took me to the hospital, where the doctors successfully reinserted my teeth into my gums.

Far from being traumatized and wanting to quit, I was so into skating and competing that the injury was just a tedious roadblock. *Mom, when can I get back on the ice? How long will it take? Will we be able to go to Nationals?*

Randy and I made it to the Oakland Nationals, but it wasn't a great competition for us. Everything felt awkward. We were lucky to do an amazing short program to music from the film *West Side Story* and win the preliminary event. Melissa and Johnny didn't have a good skate, so the judges had to put Randy and me first. But we weren't ready to be champions yet. My mom cringed in fear at the prospect. We finished second overall, the right place for us, when our long program just didn't click. I fell on a jump, and Randy turned out of a landing. Finishing second that year was one of numerous bad things that happened to us for good reasons.

We went on to Worlds in Colorado Springs and placed tenth again. The high altitude was a challenge, and we didn't perform particularly well. That was a transitional season for us in every way.

During the summer of 1975 I had another mishap. I skated past a girl who seemed to be executing a simple upright spin. I expected her to pull in, but she did the opposite. She suddenly launched herself into a camel spin, and the blade on her free foot left a gash on my thigh that went through to the muscle.

Randy saw the accident happen. I didn't look down at my leg, but I did look at Randy's face. It was white. Then Mr. Nicks came running. Fortunately he knew exactly what to do. He held the wound together to stanch the profuse bleeding. My leg took seventeen stitches that left an ugly scar. The girl whose blade had cut me felt horrible.

Fortunately Randy and I didn't have a lot of accidents and injuries. Our parents didn't worry much, because Mr. Nicks was there—and if he wasn't, someone else just as capable was there in his place. We were always protected and watched over.

As a young child, I broke my tailbone and fractured my arm, but those were minor injuries, quickly forgotten. Nothing took me off the ice for long. During our professional years I occasionally dropped out of a move. Randy and I got caught on one another sometimes, which left me dangling half up and half down. Our blades got tangled. All considered, though, we were lucky. The most dramatic wounds were the two that occurred during that awkward year when I grew.

Sometime after the second injury, I wrote a composition called "Skating." I don't remember writing it. Perhaps it was an English assignment.

In late 1975 Randy and I appeared in our first Superskates event at Madison Square Garden, a benefit for the United States Olympic Committee. We performed a sextet with JoJo Starbuck, Lisa-Marie Allen, Ken Shelley, and Linda Fratianne. Skating with JoJo and Kenny! That was such a high point in our lives, such an honor. JoJo and Kenny were always supportive of us, inviting us to visit them backstage at Ice Capades and sending cards and telegrams after all our big competitions.

It was at Superskates that we met Mr. Edwin H. Mosler Jr. He offered us a partial but generous annual sponsorship that he funneled through the USFSA, and he became a major force behind our amateur career.

Ed Mosler was the president, chairman of the board, and chief executive officer of the Mosler Safe Company that he and his brother had inherited from their father. All the commercial banks had Mosler safes. A great sports fan, Mr. Mosler was the spirit and financial bulwark behind Superskates and the United States Olympic Invitational Track Meet. He sponsored a number of skaters and baseball players. With no children of his own, he spent his life encouraging youth worldwide: athletes, scholars, and participants in the Junior Achievement program.

Mr. Mosler kept a great collection of rare mechanical coin banks in his office across the street from Madison Square Garden. He showed us shelves and shelves of banks that were housed inside illuminated glass cabinets. Mr. Mosler always made us feel really special. Everyone, according to Tai, has an angel watching over him. We had Ed Mosler.

Our second angel was Thelma Wilson, mother of Atoy, the African-American 1966 U.S. novice men's champion. Atoy skated with us at Culver Ice Arena. Later we watched him perform in professional shows. Thelma was a big supporter of ours. If we ever needed anything—skate bags, winter coats—she was there to help. There have always been certain unforgettable figures in the sport of figure skating. Thelma Wilson and Ed Mosler were two of the best.

Tai finally stopped growing. The 1975–76 season was wonderful. It was our season to win. It was strange the way the timing worked out. Melissa Militano and Johnny Johns had retired, but two other teams threatened our ascent to the national title: Alice Cook with Bill Fauver and Emily Benenson with Jack Courtney.

Although Emily and Jack were older and stronger than Tai and I were, they had placed behind us in 1975. However, the 1976 national championships were taking place in their home rink, the prestigious Broadmoor World Arena in Colorado Springs. In a sense that gave them an advantage.

I remember leaving the Broadmoor hotel with Tai and Mr. Nicks and walking around the lake to the World Arena to compete in the long program event. I knew that we had a shot at the title, but I don't recall being nervous. We had to skate extremely well to win, and we did. We were at high altitude again, and I remember being tired as we pushed through the program.

That was our first senior national title. Alice and Billy placed second. Emily and Jack were third again in spite of the home ice advantage.

I don't remember celebrating our win. With Mr. Nicks there was never much celebrating. Randy and I just went back home to California to train for the Innsbrück Olympics.

On the podium with Bill Fauver, Alice Cook, Emily Benenson, and Jack Courtney after winning our first U.S. title in Colorado Springs. (David Leonardi)

It was exciting just to be a part of those Games, to drink in the Olympic environment. I remember receiving all the free clothes designed by Halston for Sears. It was fun, but we froze. The designers and manufacturers, in choosing fabric that definitely was not wool, had apparently forgotten that Innsbrück weather was snowy and frigid. The material was red and felt-like. Our boots were rubber, not leather. Then we saw the Russians in heavy coats and sable hats!

My mom realized that we were all freezing. She and one of the team leaders went out and bought ski pants and parkas for everyone so that we could walk from place to place without getting frostbite. Even though our feet were numb in those rubber boots, walking into the stadium for the Opening Ceremonies was thrilling.

The pairs' short program, as usual, was the first skating event, and there was no pressure on us except the pressure to skate well for ourselves. We finished fifth, which was respectable.

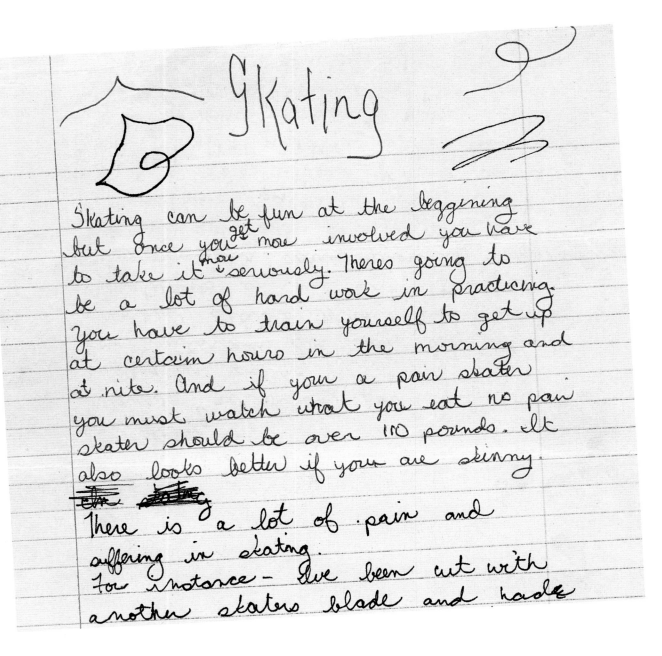

Skating

Skating can be fun at the beggining but once you get more involved you have to take it more seriously. Theres going to be a lot of hard work in practicing. You have to train yourself to get up at certain hours in the morning and at nite. And if your a pair skater you must watch what you eat no pair skater should be over 110 pounds. It also looks better if your are skinny.

There is a lot of pain and suffering in skating. For instance — I've been cut with another skaters blade and had

Essay

Skating can be fun at the beginning, but once you get more involved, you have to take it more seriously. There's going to be a lot of hard work in practicing. You have to train yourself to get up at certain hours in the morning and at night. And if you're a pairs skater, you must watch what you eat. No pairs skater should be over 110 pounds. It also looks better if you are skinny.

There is a lot of pain and suffering in skating. For instance, I've been cut with another skater's blade and had seventeen stitches in my right thigh. It was really scary when it happened, but I got over it. **Fast**. The suffering part is all in the mind, so they say. Like doing a five-minute routine set to music with certain elements you should do. It gets tiring after about the third minute but you have to push yourself. Your legs start to ache, and you start losing your breath. It's hard work, but it's worth it.

The Nicks Years

We were assigned to practice with the Japanese and the Australians. The East Germans and Russians were in other groups, but we went to watch them train, especially Irina Rodnina. It was a big thing to be in the same rink with her. The Russians didn't talk much, but I could tell that they knew what we were saying. Irina understood more English than she let on.

In recent years, whenever we've met Irina, she has always given us big hugs. She is so American now. She is an entirely different person from the quiet, withdrawn woman we first knew before the collapse of the Soviet Union.

During the long program in Innsbrück I fell on my throw double Axel—it wasn't even close—but landed my side-by-side double Axel. I flip-flopped on that jump until finally Mr. Nicks just took it out of the program. *She's not going to get it. She can't do it.* Overall we skated quite well and finished fourth for the long program, fifth overall.

The 1976 U.S. Olympic contingent: (back) Franklin S. Nelson, M.D., David Santee, Kent Weigle, Jim Millns, Hugh C. Graham Jr., M.D.; (middle) Susan Kelley, Wendy Burge, Dorothy Hamill, Judi Genovesi, Alice Cook, Colleen O'Connor, Linda Fratianne, Tai; (front) Andrew Stroukoff, Randy, Bill Fauver, Terry Kubicka.

At Innsbrück, Austria.

The Nicks Years

John Curry and Toller Cranston comprised the main event of 1976. A Soviet skater, Vladimir Kovalev, slid in between them by a strange twist of ordinals, but the competition was really all about John and Toller. John's *Don Quixote* long program was mesmerizing. It had me in tears.

Dorothy Hamill won the ladies' gold medal. Because she trained in Denver, Randy and I didn't spend much time with her over the years, although we performed with her at Ice Chips and other amateur shows. In Innsbrück we saw her only in passing, at group photo sessions and on other official occasions. She was pretty much on her own. She was on a mission. Her concentration paid off.

After Dorothy won the Olympics, she became a huge star and moved to Los Angeles. In the summertime she skated at the Santa Monica rink with us. By then, besides starring with Ice Capades, she had television specials, product endorsements, a namesake doll, and a Mercedes. We were impressed and rather proud of knowing her.

Madison Square Garden, 1977. (Margaret S. Williamson)

With our ballet teacher, Terry Rudolph.

Later Randy and I went out to dinner from time to time with Dorothy and Dean-Paul Martin, her first husband. Eventually we worked with her professionally.

A month after Innsbrück Randy and I placed fifth at the 1976 Worlds in Gothenburg, Sweden. Thanks to the Olympic coverage, we had a higher profile than ever before. We were invited to film our first television special, an episode of *The Flip Wilson Show* with Sheila Young, Peggy Fleming, Alex Karras, and Minnie Ripperton.

As the Olympic season ended, our focus changed. Rather than seek a national title, we had to defend one successfully—something skaters don't often do these days. Defending a title is harder than winning it the first time. During our four seasons as defending champions Randy and I always skated just well enough to hang on. The judges were gearing us up for 1980, I guess. They were keeping us motivated. And we were!

Our toughest competitors early in the 1976–80 Olympiad were Frank Sweiding and Gail Hamula. Then Sheryl Franks and Michael Botticelli nipped at our heels,

A *death spiral on* The Flip Wilson Show.

Our first television special, The Flip Wilson Show, *with Sheila Young, Peggy Fleming, Alex Karras, Flip Wilson, and Minnie Ripperton.*

A pairs spiral at the 1976 Worlds.

The Nicks Years

followed by Vicki Heasley and Robert Wagenhoffer and the sister-and-brother team of Peter and Kitty Carruthers. Peter and Kitty became the particular focus of attention as the change in decade approached. There was never time for Randy and me to rest on our laurels.

Our competitors weren't our rivals in a negative sense, however. Dorothy once told a story about a competitor's coach nearly running her down with a car, but most skaters kept to themselves and pursued their own goals. We stayed focused, with blinders on, and let our parents and coaches deal with collateral issues.

Randy and I continued to compete as singles through the 1977 national championships in Hartford, Connecticut, where each of us finished sixth in the senior division. Then we both stopped.

At the 1977 U.S. championships in Hartford, Connecticut, with Sheryl Franks, Michael Botticelli, Gail Hamula, and Frank Sweiding—the thrill of holding onto our title. (David Leonardi)

1977 Worlds at Tokyo, Japan

(Tony Duffy, Allsport Photographic)

(H. Yamamoto)

(H. Yamamoto)

The short program at the 1978 Worlds in Ottawa, Canada.

With Mr. Nicks at the 1979 Flaming Leaves competition (now Skate America). We were there to perform an exhibition.

The female half of a 1978 Superskates sextet: JoJo Starbuck, Lisa-Marie Allen, and me. (Margaret S. Williamson)

I hadn't done badly in singles. I was always way down in the school figures rankings, but I pulled up in the free skating event. It was the double training that was too much for me. *Okay, make a decision.* I don't remember sitting down and discussing the issue with anyone. Randy and I discussed nothing, really. It was still more a question of our parents and coach making decisions for us.

My case was easier to decide than Randy's. I knew that the change was coming, and I was so ready for it. Believe me, I did not mind giving up school figures. Without patch sessions on my schedule I didn't have to get up quite so early in the morning.

Quitting singles was not such a difficult decision for me either. I was getting tired, and I could see that maybe I wasn't ever going to do much better than sixth. That was fine. I definitely wanted to concentrate my time and attention on the pair. That was where Tai and I excelled. We were on a roll.

Although we fell short of perfection each season at the national championships, we were always in good shape and well trained. We held on to our national title in 1977 in Hartford, and again in 1978 in Portland, Maine. We also won world bronze medals both years, in Tokyo and then in Ottawa.

Our sponsor, Ed Mosler, attended all our major competitions: Nationals, Worlds, and Olympics. At Worlds he always rented a car and had us and our families chauffeured from the hotel to our events. He also took the entire entourage out to dinner to sample the cuisine of the host country. In Japan we sat on the restaurant floor and ate Kobe beef.

During the 1977–78 season, having graduated from high school, I attended USC part-time and took courses in drama, speech, and cinematography. I later studied acting privately as well. Nothing much came of the few auditions I went on. I quit college when the Olympics loomed again.

Robin Cousins

For me it all started in St. Gervais. That was my first international. It was also Tai and Randy's first, and Linda's and Charlie's. From a skating point of view, it was historic.

I had never seen Americans on ice *live* before. North Americans were brought up probably five years ahead of Europeans in confidence and independence. Specifically, the English were much more reserved. There was no comparison. I noticed that when I went to train in Denver, and I had noticed it before. The thing about the Americans was the confidence with which they skated, even when things weren't working. *The Americans are on the ice. Stand back.* It was something that they exuded.

Because of my secret desire to be a pairs skater (starting at the age of eight), I never missed pairs practices and events. I remember specifically looking at Tai and Randy and seeing equals: equal in size, equal in ability, equal in participation. It wasn't a question of the boy lugging the girl across the ice, as with the Eastern Europeans they competed against when the little-and-large era started and routines became more trick-oriented.

At one point Tai was almost taller than Randy. I thought, "It is going to be rough for them." There had to be something more, and that was very much the reason they appealed to me. It was their package. Everything was of the utmost importance: a line, a spiral, or

Taï,
May your rainbows lead
you to your chosen dream,
love always,
Robin
1979
x

Rob 79

a throw double Axel. There was never a question of one thing taking precedence over another.

John Nicks, who had started something with Kenny and JoJo, then took it that much further with Tai and Randy. I don't know that anybody else looked like them. It only worked because they had great lines. They could do the spirals and the Ina Bauers, and they were beautiful to look at. They never did anything ugly. They never did anything that didn't belong in their beautifully crafted program.

When I skated in Denver at the CIA, Scott Hamilton, Garnet Ostermaier, Simone Grigorescu, Scott Cramer, and I used to write letters to the kids in Santa Monica —Tai and Randy, Vicki Heasley, Bobby Beauchamp—

and they wrote back to us. We called the exchange Rink Wars. What awful things we would say to and about each other! I wouldn't be surprised if Tai still has one of those letters. She was, I think, easily amused, but you do find that things are so serious in the skating world. It was great to have some semblance of normality.

When I first went to California on Tom Collins's tour, Tai and Randy took me all over Los Angeles. I thought that it was the greatest thing. Shopping at the Fox Hills Mall! I had never even been to a shopping mall before.

By then, as the national champions, we received byes to skip the Southwest Pacific Sectionals, but Mr. Nicks made us do the Pacific Coast Regionals every year, even though we didn't have to, just to get our feet wet early in the season. Coasts were the chance to try out the clothes, get the number going, and iron out the bugs. It was another smart move on Mr. Nicks's part. With him we got away with nothing. Absolutely nothing!

Mr. Nicks maintained his formal demeanor throughout the decade we worked with him. Although he had an apartment, he seemed to spend most of his time at the rink. And if he wasn't there, he was likely to be on his boat, where he sometimes held little get-togethers. Once you penetrated his barrier, he was the sweetest teddy bear, but to strangers his air could be intimidating.

Santa Monica was the place to be in the summer. There was an amazing amount of skating talent under one roof. Mr. Nicks had a great group of coaches who worked with him, so skaters came from near and far: Canada, Japan, and Korea.

Paul Wylie and his pairs partner, Dana Graham, were two of the younger skaters who came to Santa Monica during our years as seniors. Dana and Paul wanted to be Tai and Randy. They were good, too, and they were evenly matched like Randy and me.

Paul idolized Randy. Everything that Randy did, Paul had to do, too. At least, he tried. He was nearly seven years younger, just a little guy, and he tried his hardest to keep up with us. That was his goal. If we went to a concert, Paul had to go to the concert. Whatever it was, Paul had to be there, too. Dana and Paul were cute, though, and we helped them out whenever we could.

Paul was amusing. He talked all the time. Yap, yap, yap, yap, yap! *What are you doing? Where are you going? Are you going to the beach? Let's go!* He was a hard worker and very bright. He skated big. Although he was short, he skated tall and long and open. He was a presence at the rink. Dana was a little more timid.

At the 1979 Nationals, Paul won the novice men's title. Dana competed in the junior ladies' event, and together they placed fifth in junior pairs. The next year they won junior pairs before Paul decided to concentrate on singles.

The best opportunities to escape our strict training regimen and have fun with our friends—even better than summers at the beach—were the ISU post-Worlds tours and the Tom Collins Tour of World and Olympic Champions that followed the ISU tour beginning in 1978. I remember running through hotel halls, knocking over ashtray stands, and playing in the elevators with Robin Cousins, Linda Fratianne, Emi Watanabe, Lisa-Marie Allen, and sometimes Charlie Tickner. Charlie was a little older than the rest of us, so he put up with us briefly, then left. We went from room to room, just hanging out. Hormones were flowing in those days, but the fun was harmless.

At Sun Valley, Idaho, with Robin Cousins. (Judy Hammond)

At Sun Valley, Idaho.

The singer Donna Summer was big. She recorded disco songs that Robin loved. He had all the tapes. He knew all the words. He was an almanac of facts about the artists. Robin had moved by then from England to America. I had a crush on him during the late 1970s.

When we weren't together, letters flew between the skaters at the Colorado Ice Arena (CIA) in Denver—Robin, Paul Wylie, and Scott Hamilton—and the skaters in Santa Monica. I still have all of those letters. They are priceless! I cherish them. Missives shot back and forth every two weeks. Maybe we were bored. Where did we get the time to write all those letters?

Robin was an amusing guy. He didn't known how to drive until he came to America to train. He learned from the Wylies, his host family in Denver. Of course, from his British point of view, we were all driving on the wrong side of the road. Once, when we were both in a Denver ice show, Robin and I went up to Red Rock, where he taught me how to drive a car with a stick shift. It was great. We jolted all the way down the road.

Linda Fratianne bore the brunt of many of Robin's and my jokes. She was goofy and gullible, a real Valley Girl. You could tell her anything, and she believed it.

As teenagers Tai and I and our skating friends traveled throughout Europe. I remember crossing the heavily guarded Russian and East German borders. Soldiers came onto the trains at the checkpoints, and we had to have our papers ready. That was nerve-wracking.

When we traveled, we usually got to sightsee a little bit between events and practices. Often the parties and dinners had themes that reflected the cultures of the host countries. Still what we saw most often were the airports, the figure skating venues, and our hotels. A number of years ago I went back to Europe as an adult. I could appreciate it so much more. *Wow, this is what Europe really looks like.*

International skating was political. There were definite blocs. The strongest was the Eastern Bloc, but Western countries had to play the game, too, in order to stay competitive.

Lisa-Marie Allen

I trained in Orange County while Tai and Randy skated in Santa Monica. In the summer months I went up once a week to take lessons from Mr. Nicks. I felt like an outsider. You just do when you come from a different rink. Tai was very shy, and so was I. Our shyness was due to insecurity and not knowing who we were. Randy was very dear and special. He and Tai would invite me to go to the coffee shop with them to have lunch.

Tai and I were so much alike that we were a perfect match as roommates on the first Tom Collins tour in 1978. Boy, did we have a good time. We played American and Canadian dates. Back then it was all of a fifteen- or sixteen-city tour that barely lasted a month.

I think that we were allowed to receive a one-hundred-dollar gift per performance, and we walked away with fifteen hundred dollars, thinking that we were rich. Today you wouldn't put on one skate for that amount of money.

Interesting things happened to Tai and me. One night in Landover, Maryland, the two of us were sleeping. We hadn't checked the lock on the connecting door between our room and the next. Someone came through the door in the middle of the night. We awakened and looked at each other, but we didn't move. We weren't sure whether or not we were dreaming. The stranger sat on my bed, then got up and left

The Nicks Years

To give an example, the West German association might say, "Get us Tai and Randy to come over and perform an exhibition at the competition we're having, and we'll get back at you." So John Nicks would send us to the West German exhibition. Sure enough, when the marks came up at subsequent competitions, Tai and I would receive good scores from the Germans and the Austrians (who were almost one and the same: a mini-bloc). Having been cooperative, we were looked upon more favorably by those associations.

Of course there was the exposure factor, too. Performing exhibitions made us more visible to European judges who would then be familiar with our strengths and abilities.

We engaged in a lot of *quid pro quo* with the British as well. It wasn't just the Soviets who played the influence game. The West was obliged to keep up. The Soviets were nastier about it, however. When they bent the rules, the ISU was scared to buck them. I see the same thing happening today.

Consider the pairs event at the 1999 Worlds in Helsinki, Finland. Two former Soviet-bloc judges were seated next to each other. CTV had a camera in the stands behind the judges' table, photographing the panel. After a particular team finished skating, one of those judges tapped the boards with his foot in a recognizable pattern. The other judge picked up the signal. When their marks came up, they had awarded the same placements. Fortunately those judges were caught and disciplined. In that respect, at least, things have changed for the better.

Randy and I attended the 2002 Salt Lake City Olympics as the guests of *Sports Illustrated*. Jamie Salé and David Pelletier were incredible in the pairs event. I thought, "Okay, the judges are going to give it to them." When that didn't happen, it felt as though the arena was going to cave in. People were livid.

I was walking out of the bathroom later when a woman came up to me, shook her ticket in my face, and said, "I paid two hundred dollars to be lied to!" That lady was pissed off. I told her, "I'm sorry. I feel exactly the way you do."

the way he had come in. I immediately locked the connecting door. Tai and I couldn't believe what had just happened.

We mentioned the incident to the hotel desk clerk.

"Oh, I don't understand how that could be. There is a minister in the adjoining room. I don't think that he would do that."

"Well, could you please confront him in the morning when he checks out?"

When questioned, the man denied having entered our room. To this day, though, I can vividly remember it, and that was more than twenty years ago. Tai and I were in separate beds, lying on our sides facing each other. Our eyes met, and we told each other wordlessly, "Don't move! This is really happening." The moral of the story is that I certainly check those locks now.

The next year Emi Watanabe was my roommate, while Tai roomed with Linda on the ISU tour that went to the Soviet Union. It was insanity, riding on trains all night. We tried to experience the Russian way of having a good time, but it just didn't agree with us young Americans. We didn't appreciate the thought of people spying on us in our hotels, and there was always a stranger sitting on the back seat of the bus, just watching us. It was all very odd.

I know that judging improprieties have been taking place as long as I've been in the sport. As an amateur you really can't say anything. But this case was so obvious. It just wasn't Elena and Anton's night—and they're brilliant. They're more lyrical than the Canadians. They're very smooth, and they're beautiful. But you can't ignore mistakes. Jamie and David just happened to be out-of-their-heads amazing. When I saw both jump combinations on a split screen, I thought, "Okay, there it is."

I was drained just sitting in the audience. I can't imagine what the skaters went through. When the Russians came out to receive their medals, you could cut the air with a knife. It was embarrassing. I told myself, "This is it. You can't make people pay that much money for tickets and then lie to them. Our sport is in so much trouble right now."

When I got home, I asked, "Mom, was what happened with Randy and me in Lake Placid as dramatic as what's going on now?" She answered, "Yes, but it was a different drama."

During the 1978–79 season Tai and I won Pacific Coasts, successfully defended our U.S. title in Cincinnati, Ohio, then went on to Vienna, Austria, for the world championships.

We had good practices in Vienna, but we knew that the field was tight, even without Rodnina and Zaitsev, who were expecting their first child, a son, Sasha, in about a month. The Russian team of Sergei Shakhrai and Marina Cherkasova, a "one-and-one-half" pair, offered us strong opposition. So did the East Germans, Sabine Baess and Tassilo Thierbach. Tai and I won the short program, but barely. We skated clean, but we didn't finish very far ahead.

The opening of our long program was from *The Planets* by Tomita. I can't remember the slow section, but we finished to Hungarian dances. I felt my skate lace come undone going into the last minute. *Oh, God. Come on. Hold on there.* Fortunately I was wearing a boot cover that kept the lace together.

We hit our routine: throw triple Salchow, split double twist, swan lift into star lift, side-by-side double flips, throw double Axel, cartwheel lift. The program was *on*. It was our out-of-body experience. Every athlete has a best event. He might approach that level again, but he can never top it. Vienna was our magical moment.

Linda Fratianne

My first memory of Tai is from the Los Angeles Figure Skating Club show at the Pickwick rink in Burbank. We both had braces and were going through that awkward stage. A little bit later, when Tai and Randy were with Mr. Nicks, I saw them every Sunday when I skated in Santa Monica.

When we all went to St. Gervais in 1973, I had a huge crush on Randy. I was terribly shy back then. To let him know that I liked him was completely out of the question. Oh, that dark hair and those big, blue eyes! I didn't really know him, but I thought that he was cute, and I admired his great skating.

My mother eventually became a good friend of Randy's mother. She kept her abreast of my activities and vice versa. On our ISU tour in 1979, my father and Tai's mother were the chaperons on an incredible ten-day trip to Moscow, Kiev, and Leningrad.

A drawing by Robin Cousins.

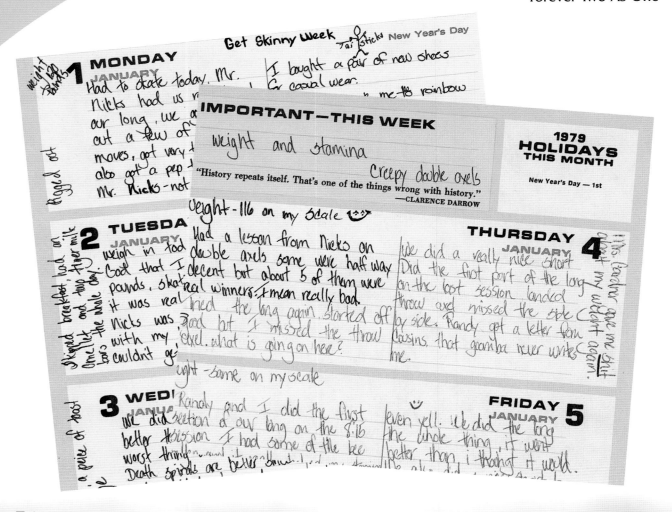

Tai

Ten Days until Coasts: Get Skinny Week

Monday, January 1: Weight 120 pounds. Pigged out. Had to skate today. Mr. Nicks had us run through our long. We got to leave out a few of the hard moves. Got very tired—still. Also got a pep talk from Mr. Nicks. Not too heavy. I bought a pair of new shoes for casual wear. Sharon Dror gave me two rainbow decals. Really pretty. Watched myself on TV. Wow. Daydreamed about growing two more inches. How nice it would be. 5' 7.

Tuesday, January 2: Skipped breakfast. Had an omelet and two Tiger Milk bars the whole day. Weigh in today. I pray to God that I lose a few pounds. Skated really shitty. It was really awful. Mr. Nicks was not too impressed with my little show. I couldn't get through the program. I weighed in and actually lost something. I'm still too big for my partner, though. Saw my brother today. He looked great. I wish he still lived here at home. I miss his friends also. Daydreamed about the Masons in Hawaii. I miss them a great deal.

Wednesday, January 3: Two eggs, a piece of toast, one orange. We did our short. It was better than yesterday. The worst thing was the lasso lift. Death spirals are better since I got my blades sharpened. The long is getting better, but I still have trouble with stamina. Interview with Elizabeth Wheeler. Really boring and not much fun. Also went to Mrs. Fox's and saw my new outfits. Really nice. Talked to Jill Strawbridge for an hour. Bacon and cheese omelet for dinner.

Thursday, January 4: Weight 116 on my scale. Two eggs and piece of toast. Mrs. Gardner gave me shit about my weight again. Had a lesson from Nicks on double Axels. Some were halfway decent but about five of them were real winners. I mean really bad. Tried the long again. Started off good but I missed the throw Axel. What is going on here? We did a really nice short. Did the first part of the long on the last session. Landed throw Axel, missed the side-by-side. On the last session landed a throw Axel, missed a side-by-side. Randy got a letter from Cousins. That goomba never writes me.

The Nicks Years

I think that Tai and I were the last pair to skate. There is a picture of us hugging as we came off the ice. We knew that we had won. We had been first going into the long program event, and we had skated very well, so what else could the judges do with us?

Believe it or not, Randy and I had never hugged each other before. We were pretty buttoned down. Even that night we didn't show much emotion until the long program ended. Then we waved to the audience, turned to face Mr. Nicks, and embraced each other. That was a great hug.

The fact that Randy and I never got too excited had a lot to do with Mr. Nicks. "Don't get flighty and uppity," he would say, "because you have a hard year ahead of you. You don't know the work that you are in for."

Mr. Nicks kept us grounded. I thank him for that. He was very controlled himself. He certainly didn't jump up and down while we performed. In Vienna we caught a glimpse of him during the last section of our long program when we had just a minute left to go. He gave us a little sign of encouragement, but that was the most excitement he displayed. Even though he stayed cool on the outside, however, I noticed that he went through great quantities of Tums.

Randy and I did scream for joy when we got a 6.0 from the West German judge. There were six 5.9s. That was a wonderful moment. Still we didn't go nuts. Now I look back at that night and realize that it was pretty perfect. It was great. It was our moment. It was the performance of our amateur career. My dad was up in the press booth taking pictures, and he cried. The tough detective sergeant cried.

Friday, January 5: Two eggs and piece of toast. Weight—same on my scale. Randy and I did the first section of our long on the 8:15 session. I had some of the bee pollen and it really helped my stamina a lot. I landed the throw double Axel finally but again missed the side-by-side. Mr. Nicks didn't even yell. We did the long. The whole thing. It went better than I thought it would. We also did a nice short.

Saturday, January 6: Went shopping with Jodi. I got my new Nikes and went to see Steve at the Warehouse. I think I'm in love with him again. Ate dinner at Jodi's house. Went home and watched S.N.L.

Sunday, January 7: Take pictures in front of the Music Center 1:30. Randy called and said the Zam was broken. Went to the rink early. Randy had our new outfits so we tried them out. Short was fine. Long a little short in the body.

Monday, January 8: Got to the rink late because of traffic, but I didn't get in trouble. Went through long again. I missed the same two things again. I know it's mental because they're both fine in practice. Short was good today. Got home and packed for Coasts. I can't believe another year is starting. Oh well! I miss my brother.

Tuesday, January 9: Went in at 6:30 but didn't skate. Had a lesson. Randy and I fell on our lasso. I killed my hip and I think Randy hurt his thigh. We will do our long at ten. Long went great. Finally landed the throw Axel. Missed the side-by-side again. Made it to Santa Rosa. We skated at eight o'clock with the dancers. Real fun. Just did parts of our program.

Wednesday, January 10: Pacific Coasts start. Mr. Nicks picked us all up at six and then we drove to Cupertino. Practiced there until one or so, then drove to Sausalito for lunch. Then went home. It's pouring rain outside.

*Just before the short program at the 1979 Worlds in Vienna,
I was cracking my knuckles, a habit I got from Randy.*

The Nicks Years

My mother was up in the stands, but Randy's mother always stayed in the bathroom while we competed. She couldn't handle the tension.

After our performance, the spectators rose to their feet. There were many Americans in the audience. I didn't cry on the podium. I didn't remind myself, "We made history! We're the first American pair to win the world title since Karol and Peter Kennedy won it in 1950." That realization didn't enter my mind. What my inner voice said was, "I didn't fall! I may have had a little trip, but I landed everything, and I *did not fall*."

Randy and I looked at each other and giggled. We were so relieved that our quest was over, that we had done what we had trained so hard to do. The work had all paid off. And Mr. Nicks was happy with us.

Unbeknownst to us, Mr. Mosler did the most amazing thing after we won the competition. He scooped up the Zamboni ice scrapings and put them in a container for their flight back to the United States. Later he had Tiffany's seal the melted ice into two Baccarat crystal jars. Thanks to Mr. Mosler, we still have the actual water molecules on which we won Worlds. Randy's supply is starting to evaporate a little. He needs to take the container somewhere to be resealed.

Mr. Mosler threw a party for us at the official hotel. Then we had time to relax until the exhibitions, where we performed to a disco version of "Over the Rainbow." That was fun, but we didn't get too full of ourselves.

Then we left Vienna for a small ISU tour. At Wembley Arena we met Queen Elizabeth II. For some reason I gave her my flowers. She looked to me as though she wanted to hold something. There she was with her little purse, as fair-skinned as a porcelain doll.

I don't think that the 1980 Olympics could ever have topped our experience in Vienna. We would have competed with essentially the same long program. In my heart I don't believe that events were meant to play out in exactly the same way again, especially not with all the pressures of 1980.

A month after we won Worlds I received a humorous letter of congratulations from Scott Hamilton. The last line mentioned "sex, drugs, and alcohol." I recently told Scott that in retrospect I found his words ironic.

"Isn't it funny what happened in my life after that? You must have *known* something."

John Nicks

In Vienna Tai and Randy had led quite convincingly in the short program. I began to understand, about two-thirds of the way through their long program, that they had the world championship won. All they had to do was perform the last minute and one-half well. I knew that they were very capable of that. The risky, dangerous elements had been completed, so I started to have a good feeling, as a lot of other coaches have had about other skaters. When Brian Boitano won his wonderful

Olympic gold medal in 1980, it was apparent during the last minute that he knew he had it won. You could see him change. My feelings were similar in Vienna.

I really enjoyed my years with Tai and Randy. We still have a close relationship, and it is always very good to see them. I am so pleased that they have kept their careers going. The last time I saw them skate, it wasn't bad at all!

At the Vienna Worlds with Sabine Baess, Tassilo Thierbach, Marina Cherkasova, and Sergei Shakhrai.

Our last U.S. competition, at the 1980 Nationals in Atlanta, Georgia, was the most difficult for us. Although we made some technical errors, I believe that we deserved to win, but we didn't give our best performance. I made a mistake on the throw double Axel, and Randy didn't bring me down smoothly from our one-handed lift. Still we received all seven first placements.

We had known that the event would be mentally tough and highly competitive because of the upcoming Lake Placid Olympics, and it was certainly our most nerve-wracking title defense.

The same thing happened to Linda and Charlie. None of us skated well in Atlanta. Luckily we all kept our titles and went to Lake Placid as national champions.

The 1980 Olympic Games were an icebreaker for Tai and me. They marked a definite change in our relationship. We had attained maturity, we were about to make a change in our careers, and for the first time we had to reach decisions together as adults. There were certain issues that only we could deal with. We were on our own, and we began to grow closer to each other as a result.

On the podium with our world gold medals. We have perspiration under our arms. We really worked that night.
(Bruno Schlatter, AP Wirephoto)

A great hug in Vienna.

Meeting Queen Elizabeth II on the 1979 world tour at Wembley Arena with Natalia Linichuk, Gennadi Karponosov, and Vladimir Kovalev. (Tony Duffy, Allsport Photographic)

We had expected to go on from the Olympics to the world championships in Dortmund, West Germany. However, I wasn't able to resume skating until two weeks prior to Worlds, and my injury still hurt. Fortunately I knew that if I kept going to therapy and gradually building my strength, I would be fine in the long run.

On March 7, 1980, Tai and I announced our withdrawal from the Worlds roster. At that point we knew that we were going to join Ice Capades soon. Ironically Rodnina and Zaitsev also withdrew, just days before Worlds, reporting that Irina had a shoulder injury.

Randy and I didn't have a manager, although we received offers from potential candidates. I remember going to many meetings here in Los Angeles, but there was no one we really liked among the group of managers we met during that time. Mr. Nicks acted as our advisor, which was probably the best thing for us. It was scary to be approached by people with big ideas. *You are going to be huge stars!*

We were contractually bound to tour with Ice Capades for three years, so there was really no sense in hiring a manager. Our work was cut out for us.

We did engage a publicist, though. As a result Randy and I were hired for an odd and interesting assortment of jobs. We judged the World Roller Disco Championships in Inglewood. We posed for print ads for Polar Sport and Sun Life. We appeared with Burt Reynolds and Dom DeLuise at the Los Angeles Press Club Awards (and laughed hysterically all evening). On *The Mike Douglas Show* we taught Mike, actor Lee Marvin, and rocker Ted Nugent how to roller-skate. Surprisingly we weren't at all shy around other entertainers, probably because they weren't shy with us.

Randy and I appeared on many talk shows right after the Olympics, and the hosts asked the same questions every time. "Tai, what were you feeling? Randy, what were *you* feeling?" Our responses became highly programmed. Before our press conference

Scott Hamilton

I've known Tai and Randy forever. I watched them grow up. Randy was the alpha dog in the group: dynamic and outgoing. Of the two, he was the vocal one.

All the guys had crushes on Tai. I was one of those guys. She was always laughing, funny, and friendly. I don't remember her ever telling a joke, but she laughed at everyone else's. She was a good audience.

I first met them in 1970, when I went to skate in the Golden West competition in Culver City. There were only two ice dance couples in the low-level event, so I was paired up with a girl who was there, and we put together a free dance in a day and a half. I had taken her through her dance tests, and we thought, "Wow, we can get another award if we enter the event." We came in third and got our trophies.

I saw Tai and Randy at all the competition parties. There were pictures of them on the walls of the rink.

People thought that they were going to accomplish great things, even though they were only about ten and twelve years old at the time.

Randy and Robin Cousins were good friends. They started the Rink Wars thing, and we all kept it going. Because Tai and Randy were in California and I was in Colorado most of the time, we never crossed paths except at training camps and a couple of mini-tours that we did together.

Randy, John Nicks, and I shared a room on one of those tours. Randy and I went out late to get something to eat. When we came back, Mr. Nicks was already asleep. Whenever we went to international events in Europe, it was tight quarters. The beds were all pushed together. Mr. Nicks's arm and leg were lying across several beds.

Mr. Nicks was a very serious guy. We didn't want to

The medal ceremony in Vienna, 1979. The flags flanking ours are East German and Soviet.

wake him up, and we certainly didn't want to touch him accidentally while we were sleeping. Randy and I laughed so hard that night, trying to avoid Mr. Nicks's stray limbs.

I was the little low-level skater while Tai and Randy were taking off and having a lot of success. They were the ones close to my age who made it big before I ever had aspirations of doing anything on an international scale. Then I made the 1978 world team and the 1980 Olympic team. Those were the times when Tai and Randy were at the height of their popularity as national champions. Every four years there are lead people in men's, ladies', pairs, and dance. Tai and Randy were the elite, the most popular, during that Olympiad, along with Charlie Tickner and Linda Fratianne. That was a pretty strong group.

I wasn't entertainment-industry savvy. Tai and Randy

were. They were beautifully produced. They had the right costumes. They had announcements at the beginning of their programs: "United States Champions Tai Babilonia and Randy Gardner." When I heard that, I always said, "Wow, that's really cool. How did they do that?" I admired the fact that they seemed to be so put together.

Tai and Randy were a product of Los Angeles and later of the Ice Capades system. If I had to edit my program, it was like an audible anvil on top of your head. We lived in two different worlds. I was very unsophisticated. I kind of invented myself. I never really fit into a specific mold. I knew that, in order to succeed, I needed to present myself, so basically that's what I did. They did the same thing, but they had access to the upper echelon of the entertainment industry.

in Lake Placid, Mr. Nicks had told us what to say and what not to say. I guess that his words stuck with us, because we always said the same things.

Even today I tend to make those same comments when someone brings up the subject of Lake Placid. I tell myself, "Don't get deep with anyone." Many talk shows allow guests only two or three minutes of real conversation, and that time goes by quickly. I have always preferred the shows with longer segments that allow us to settle in and answer questions more comprehensively.

After the Olympics I met a guy—for the first time. Linda Fratianne threw a big bash at her house and invited all her friends. Some of them were actors.

Linda was on a high after winning the ladies' silver medal, but I felt a little down. I wasn't really sad, although I wasn't having a great time, either. I was just sitting alone for the most part, nursing a drink, when I noticed someone staring at me. It was the middle brother on *The Brady Bunch*, the cute one, "Peter."

Christopher Knight lived in Chatsworth, in the San Fernando Valley. We started going out. I had that electric feeling, the one that you get when the phone rings and you run to answer it before anyone else can. *No, Mom, it's okay. I'll get it!* He was my first love.

In May Randy and I took part in filming "Bob Hope's All-Star Comedy Birthday Party" at the Air Force Academy in Colorado Springs. It was Bob's seventy-seventh

A Letter from Scott Hamilton

4-17-79

Dear Tai,

How are ya? I hope everything is great, and I would like to express my sincerest congratulations on becoming the world champions, and also I would like to convey that you two were the best, and I am proud of you. My only regret is that I couldn't be there with you.

So how's your life? It must be great, and you can tell me all about it real soon. If you are doing the Denver show, I have sooo much to tell you.

I talked to X last night, and it was so good to hear her voice. I am really missing her. She is the only normal one in Denver, and except for an occasional mother malfunction, she is the most fun, too. She sounds really happy and didn't talk about Randy *too* much. It was kinda funny the way we talked. It was like a two-way Dear Abby. I gave advice, and she gave advice and expressed concern and at times was a little surprised with a few things that happened this spring. But, as it turned out, we got everything all straightened out and hung up just that much more confused than when we started.

Are you guys coming to Squaw Valley? Except for nine or ten Munchkins, it will be great. And except for the exercise class, the testing and skating, it will be better than ever. Can't wait, or maybe I can. I am going to feel real strange going with a different pro.

Oh well, take it real easy and watch out for all those wild and crazy times in life that make it worth living, like sex, drugs, alcohol and *Saturday Night Live*.

I love ya and write me,

Scott

P.S. Tai Babilonia is sooo tall that she can stand in Wyoming and see the Golden Gate Bridge.

birthday, and I enjoyed meeting him and his wife, Dolores. Randy and I later stayed several times at their house in Palm Springs. It looked like a spaceship, built in the round on the side of a mountain, with a courtyard in the middle and a mushroom-like dome over the top.

In June Randy and I took a two-week vacation. Randy went to New York City, while I flew to Hawaii. I had most of the rest of the summer off, too, and my romance with Christopher bloomed quickly. There were lots of beach parties. I had never hung out with a *guy* before (except Randy, of course). It was a neat feeling. I suppose that I needed someone who wasn't a skater. There were other things to talk about. He had seen what happened in Lake Placid, and he took care of me. There was no pressure to do this or do that—except to hang out and have fun.

I learned something from each and every guy I ever dated. There was always something that I took home, positive or negative. From Christopher Knight I learned that I wasn't ready for a relationship. I met him, and then I had to leave.

Christopher Knight

I had a friend who knew Linda Fratianne. We all grew up in the Valley. I must admit that I'm not an ice skating aficionado, other than following it casually, but Tai and Randy certainly were a special duo on the ice. I was aware of them because of all the pre-Olympic publicity that surrounded them as Americans who were touted as potential medal winners. I believe that Linda's party was set up before the Olympics, so I knew that there was a chance that I was going to get to meet Tai, and I followed the Olympics very closely.

Lo and behold, there she was at the party, standing across the room with that smile that can melt. At the risk of sounding corny, she looked virginal. I was smitten immediately.

Tai and I started dating. I always showed up at the skating rink when she practiced. It was all I could do not to think about her. There was a day that I remember as one of the most perfect days of my life. In the pile of days that one has lived, that one stands out. It was a day at the beach with Tai and some of her skating friends. We partied a little bit, but it was innocent—just some beer. I was never really a heavy partier. I don't know what it was about that day, but it was magical.

I had no idea until we got reacquainted recently that the relationship that we were able to develop over two and one-half or three months had the impact on Tai that it did. It wasn't a consummated love, but I felt for her deeply. Because of where I came from, I anticipated what she was about to go through. She was embarking on the part of her career that would presumably justify all the years of sacrifice. Yet it seemed, from what I gathered, that it wasn't going to be a pleasant experience for her. There was an awful lot that she was suddenly going to have to confront with very little basis for dealing with it.

I don't think that it matters who you are—child actor, skater, gymnast. The sacrifices of time can be similar. You have only one childhood, and it can easily be taken away because it's so short. Every year is vital. I'm not a proponent of children working—not that Tai had been "working." She had been going after a dream. But it wasn't clear to me whether or not it had been her dream or one that others had formed for her, and had pushed her to form, because of her talent and because she was in the right place at the right time. She seemed to me to be slightly uncomfortable, as though she really had no idea what *her* dream was.

A lot of Tai's confusion could have been due to what happened in Lake Placid. That had been the dream, and it had blown up. Making money was more or less the next avenue after the dream to make all the sacrifice make sense, but Tai wasn't in a position yet to be a business owner, and she *was* a business at that point. It seemed to me as though that was when her missed childhood should have started—and it did, in a way, but unfortunately under a public spotlight and with too many responsibilities, at a time when I think she really needed to decompress and relax.

Nonetheless those things do happen, and the sequence was well known beforehand. Tai totally recognized how lucky she was to be in her position, but she was a sweet, naïve, inexperienced girl and not yet a woman. People were going to take their bites out of her, and she didn't

When I went on the road with Ice Capades, I told myself, "Okay, I'll be gone for nine months. When I come back, though, we'll be together." It was hard to keep our relationship going by telephone, and I came home a completely different person. Our timing was bad. I was too young. I was just not ready.

Christopher was a wonderful friend, though. He protected me. I felt very safe with him after all that I had been through during my amateur skating career and especially during the months surrounding the Olympics.

have any of the armor necessary to weather that well, in my estimation. Becoming her own person was going to be difficult in light of all the pressures around her. She hadn't really exercised her own muscle yet. She had always done what other people wanted her to do.

I got to know rather quickly how innocent Tai was and how easily misguided she could perhaps find herself. I was certainly not going to be the person to take advantage of her. Not knowing me, though, Tai's mom and other people around her adopted a carefully standoffish attitude toward me, so I knew that there were others trying to protect her.

Randy was obviously a very important person in her life. He was like a brother. A lot of Tai's motivation had to do with the desire not to disappoint Randy and not to disappoint her parents. She thought very little about herself. What did Tai want? I tried to give her whatever little bit of guidance I could. I was two years older and had some experience, but I couldn't offer a whole lot.

Our relationship was her opportunity for a short period of time to do what she wanted to do. But make no mistake about it, it was obvious that she wasn't going to have any more than those three months to do so before she embarked on the moneymaking route. The fame and all the attention that comes with it were things that I had been all too accustomed to, and I felt akin to Tai as a person, as a soul. Fame and attention are more confusing than they are healthful.

I knew what I was getting myself into with Tai. Our three-month infatuation was doomed from the very beginning. I knew that I was going to get crushed, so when I did get crushed, it wasn't as though I could hold

it against her. She just didn't have any choice in the matter.

But it frustrated me that somebody was going to live a life for others the way she was about to. Luckily there was a legacy and a benefit: the financial means that she gathered from it. But it was so apparent that she could be taken advantage of. She had been totally protected in an artificial environment, working hard and deriving very little status from it. All of a sudden she was being released into the world on her own.

So Tai was about to go off and have an interesting life. I would go my way, and she would go hers. I wasn't in a position to make a long-term commitment, and I wasn't interested in doing so. What was left was an adolescent romance, and those are not of consequence enough to endure the kind of separation that we faced. Nor was what Tai was about to go through appealing to me—all the attention—but it was clear that I couldn't protect her.

Off she went. No sooner did she go off than I started reading about her and Andy Gibb. I thought, "Yep, there you go. It's starting." It is very easy to be enamored of all the popularity. The new friends that you can make are already celebrities, and now you are part of that crowd. That might be interesting, but it's certainly not nourishing.

chapter four

Tai's Lost Decade

Our first Harry Langdon studio portrait, shot during the summer of 1980. We've used him ever since. He lays down a clear piece of plastic that looks like ice. Then he makes fog all around it. We always have fun during the shoots. Over the years Harry has captured so many changes, so many different looks. My hair has been various shades. It has been both short and long. I've had bangs. Randy has basically stayed the same. (Harry Langdon)

Randy and I signed with Ice Capades on April 1, 1980. Two days later we held a press conference to announce the signing. It was only that week that Randy's physical condition returned to 100 percent.

Our agreement ran to the millions, the last of the big contracts. We were exclusive to Ice Capades. That meant that the company had us pretty well locked up, although with permission we could step out to do television shows and commercials.

The company let us open at home at the Los Angeles Sports Arena between April 15 and 27. Then we played the Long Beach Arena from April 29 through May 4. Those were the best three weeks of my Ice Capades career. It was all so new. We were fresh, eager, and just happy to be skating together at all. We knew that we had peaked as amateurs. There was nothing more that we could accomplish in that domain. It was time for our next chapter.

Randy and I performed to *Don Quixote*, the slow section of our long program, and to "The Flight of the Phoenix." The show was always sold out, and the audiences went nuts over us. People stood as soon as our names were announced—even before we skated out onto the ice. That had never happened to us before. The nicest thing for me was being able to live at home some of the time and drive myself to the arena. Life seemed normal again.

In September our show officially opened in Duluth, Minnesota, as Ice Capades East Company did every year. (The following season we skated primarily with West Company. After that we split our time half-and-half.)

We were signed on as guest stars for thirty weeks per season on average, almost the full tour. I loved the work, but it was hard. At each performance Tai and I skated two pairs cold spots and a solo each. The company booked our schedule, chose our music, and made our costumes (until the third year, when we went to Hollywood designer Jef Billings on our own). If we wanted to, we could sit with management and present suggestions. Sometimes the bosses accepted our ideas. Sometimes they didn't.

We were obligated to do publicity, and the company worked us hard. We gave a press conference in each city as well as many interviews. Sometimes there were as many as eight publicity calls a day, either live or by phone, with newspapers, radio, and TV. That kept us very busy.

We opened in a new city on either Tuesday or Wednesday, so Mondays and sometimes Tuesdays were travel days and days off. That was when we did our laundry. I used the hotel laundry service or went to the Laundromat with a group of chorus skaters. It wasn't glamorous.

We usually rode buses between cities, carrying our luggage down to the hotel lobby in time for an 8:00 or 8:30 A.M. pick-up. The trips were rarely more than five hours long. Tai and I sometimes jumped from one company to another. Depending on the distance, we might fly from show to show.

Our first day with Ice Capades in Duluth. The button is perfect: "We Love Ice Capades." It was downhill from there.

Tai's Lost Decade

Each of the three companies included thirty chorus skaters: mostly Americans, a few French-Canadians, and a smattering of Europeans. Some of them treated us as stars, some were intimidated by us, some were jealous, and some became our friends.

I liked the lifestyle, being a part of the company. I think that I appreciated it more than Tai did. As the stars of the show we made great money. Yes, there were management problems that we had to deal with, and the physical grind was something that I couldn't handle nowadays, but I appreciated what we learned from the structure, as skaters and as performers. Costume fittings, publicity calls, meetings with the producers, directors, and choreographers: those were good ways of learning about the business.

Living on the road was difficult for me. It was as though someone had kicked me in the face. I didn't even know how to balance a checkbook. We fended for ourselves. If we didn't retrieve our luggage, it remained out by the bus. We learned responsibility. I didn't know that tour life would be like that. Before we began, I told myself, "We are the stars of the show. We will be treated like stars." We were, to some extent. I had just imagined that there would be more to it. I don't know what I expected.

We were on the road for nine months out of the year, two weeks off at Christmas, a new city every week. I had my twenty-first birthday on a bus on the way from Duluth to Pittsburgh.

Going into Ice Capades, I had thought that the performance aspect would be easy: only a few numbers a night. But performing was hard. I didn't know how to be a good professional.

In November, during a break from Ice Capades, Randy and I traveled to Beijing to film "United States Figure Skaters in China." It was a groundbreaking visit by western performers, televised on ABC's *Wide World of Sports*. Peggy Fleming, JoJo Starbuck, Ken Shelley, Lisa-Marie Allen, Charlie Tickner, and Linda Fratianne went on that trip with us. What I remember most was that the time passed so quickly that it felt as though we were there one minute and gone the next.

We did have the opportunity to visit some palaces, walk on the Great Wall, and eat at a few good restaurants, but I was tired, and my skating performance wasn't great. I couldn't get my feet under me. As soon as I became acclimated, we left. *What was that? Was that China?*

A Poem by Tai

few tears

lived a strange protected life
on ice for many years
sheltered world i did depart
surprisingly few tears

8/9/82

During the first year with Ice Capades my skating was okay. During the second and third years, though, I didn't skate well. I skipped shows. I was just not on top of things. I became overweight. At first the audiences were warm. Later they caught on. The reviewers caught on, too. The Lake Placid aura was gone, along with my innocence. I had left them in some nameless, faceless city on the tour. The company expected more from me than I gave, but I just didn't have any more to give.

I tried. I practiced for several hours a day before each show. Randy was enjoying himself, and I didn't let him know how unhappy I was. But the heads of the company must have known that something was up when they saw the product that I gave them.

My contract required me to do throw double Axels, but I missed them more often than I landed them. I completed maybe two a week. I tried, fell, sprawled, and then cried afterward. I was hard on myself. *Why can't I do this every night, three shows on Saturday and two on Sunday? Why can't I do it?* Once in a while the company flew in Mr. Nicks, who attempted to fix the problem. It never got fixed. The real problem was my state of mind.

The principal skaters played second fiddle to the characters. The Smurfs, in our third year, did bang-up business. The kids in the audience were obviously there to see them, not us. After the Smurfs finished performing, the children threw tributes onto the ice—whatever objects they could find close at hand. The ice surface was always a mess, but Randy and I were the ones who followed the Smurfs.

I had a private room in every hotel. I didn't feel that I had much in common with the chorus skaters. They hadn't gone through what Randy and I had as amateurs. Some had competed, but they hadn't taken competitive skating to our level. We were a different breed. It took time to figure out the touring world. The other female principals had boyfriends. Some of those boyfriends were in the show with us. I just didn't go there.

At the Bob Hope birthday special, Randy and I had met Loni Anderson, Diana Ross, Barbara Mandrel, and Andy Gibb. Andy, younger brother of the Bee Gees, was twenty-two. I was nineteen. Within a year he and I were dating.

Andy Gibb was such a dear person, so young, so giving, so vulnerable. He would have given his last dime to anyone who needed it. From Andy I learned about the power of publicity. He had it down. I believe that he enjoyed seeing his name in headlines. That was good for his career. But suddenly I started seeing my name, too. Yes, we were dating. But it was pretty wild to open up a magazine and learn that Andy

Sarah Kawahara

I was performing in the Ice Capades when Tai and Randy were brought in for the last couple of cities in 1980 to make their professional début. They were very willing to please—and usually very quiet.

Ice Capades had a standard routine. New pros were always asked to address the audience before one of their two numbers, so Tai and Randy had to learn to speak in public. I remember that Tai practically screamed into the microphone until she got her volume modulated.

Although Tai wasn't underage, she was young enough that Ice Capades felt that they had to assign a chorus skater to escort her and act as a companion. They needed to provide a supportive buddy to help her assimilate. Randy was more social.

With Bryant Gumbel on Today.

Backstage with Stevie Nicks.

Meeting celebrities

Andy Gibb in 1981.

With Burt Reynolds at the Los Angeles Press Club Awards.

With Oleg and Ludmila Protopopov.

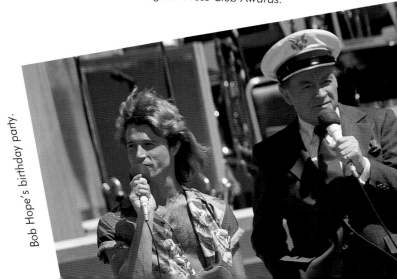
Bob Hope's birthday party.

and I were "getting married." I don't know how that kind of rumor starts. I was on the road most of the time. However, I learned very quickly that publicity is powerful, and the public is willing to believe almost anything.

I didn't seek out famous people. Based in Los Angeles, I found it hard to get away from them. I never looked for any of it. Adventure somehow found *me*.

All of a sudden large numbers of people were unnaturally friendly to Randy and me. That was shocking. I wasn't used to it. Rather than enjoying the attention, I wondered about people's motivations. Who were my *real* friends? I couldn't tell if people were trying to be friendly only because I was half of Tai and Randy, the headline act of their show. I really didn't know.

Randy was my closest friend in the show, although we didn't often socialize together. Even though we had the comfortable closeness of people with a long history together, as troubled as I was, I didn't confide in him. And if he saw signs of trouble, he didn't acknowledge them. He went into denial. That was how he protected himself. Since I didn't latch onto anyone else, I lived as a loner.

I know that the company worried about me. I would get into a city and go off on my own. I never called any of the other girls to say, "Let's go shopping." It was always me alone, hunting for antiques. Sometimes I locked myself in my room and did a little writing. I guess that those were my ways of dealing with the fear of sharing myself with others.

Richard Ewell, our childhood friend, was with the show during our first year. It was neat to have him there. He did as much for me as he could, but he had to worry about himself, too.

Randy was much better at adapting to Ice Capades than I was. He was a little older, and mentally he was *there* before I was. He was ready for touring life. I had assumed that I was ready for it, too, but clearly I wasn't.

I developed trouble sleeping at night. The performance director suggested, "Have a glass of wine. It's the perfect sleep aid."

"Okay, I'll try it," I said, and I really liked it. I enjoyed the feeling that the wine induced. It made me sleepy, but it also made everything seem better. It numbed all my unhappiness. When the wine wasn't strong enough, I found harder stuff.

My contract specified a certain weight that I had to maintain to avoid being fined. There was a look that went along with Ice Capades, a professional showgirl look. The costumes were only *this big*. I was always over my limit, and I was not the only one. Diet pills—amphetamines, "speed"—made the rounds of the company. I started taking them to lose a few pounds, and I usually dropped just enough to make my weight for the weigh-in. I would do anything to avoid getting those awful pink slips under my door. They were my greatest humiliation.

During our second and third years with Ice Capades my weight became a problem for Randy. I was harder to lift than I had been during our amateur days. Instead of

Our 1983 program insert.

The victim of a practical jokester.

Ice Capades

Our 1980 program insert.

With Lisa-Marie Allen and Charlie Tickner.

Our trunks in the hall.

Talking to the audience at our début.

Presenting our 1979 long program costumes to the Smithsonian. (Richard Hofmeister)

Poem by Tai

suffer for your art ... thank you, Mabel

touring with this show is sometimes
very rough
though life out of a suitcase made
me kind of tough
experiencing growing up
every other day
walking unfamiliar streets
god! i miss l.a.
sweet and innocent all the time
tends to be a strain
plastic people pretend to know me
smile through the pain
performing is my magical moment
spotlights bright and quick
"suffer for your art," she said
it somehow did the trick

Somewhere on the road with Ice Capades
10/11/81

dieting sensibly, I abused both diet pills and alcohol. I guess that I had an addictive personality. I can't imagine what my body went through with the combination of diet pills, drinking, and insufficient food.

There were several anorexic girls in the company. I didn't know what anorexia was. *How do you stay so skinny?* That was just part of the lifestyle.

There was always social drinking when the group went out together, and I wanted to keep up. I was "legal." I was free. My parents weren't there. I was a *big* girl. In public, at least, I gradually broke out of my shell. I suspect that drinking had a great deal to do with that. Drinking numbs the pain and makes you feel fearless. You don't really know what you are doing, so you take chances.

If anyone wanted to help me, I wasn't ready for it. I honestly believed that I could manage on my own. The company bosses did the best that they could. There was only so much that they could do. Solving my problems was up to me, and I didn't understand that yet.

On The Mike Douglas Show *with Mike, Ted Nugent, and Lee Marvin.*

With Elton John in October 1980.

I don't think that I'm the smartest person in the world. At least, I never was the smartest in school. But I became streetwise during Ice Capades. As hard as it was, that three- or four-year period was like the high school experience that I never had. It was a great learning opportunity, something that I *had* to go through. It made me tough and guarded. There were so many nights when I wanted to go home, when I didn't know what to do. I'm glad that I didn't bail out.

One night in Cleveland Randy and I attended Elton John's show. Ice Capades was opening the next night in the same venue. Elton dedicated "Rocket Man" to us. That was amazing. When I ran into him again in the 1990s, I told him, "Elton, it's great to see you again." He replied, "Yes, it's nice being coherent this time around, isn't it?" I agreed that it was. We were both in a much better space than a decade earlier.

During our fourth year of professional skating, Randy and I performed with Ice Capades on a limited basis. That was more manageable. After I left full-time touring behind, I finally *got* it: I had a great job. That knowledge didn't hit me until the treadmill slowed.

During the 1981–82 season, a little over a year after the Olympics, Tai and I got a one-shot acting job on a children's television show, *The Great Space Coaster*. That's where we met Emily Bindiger. She became an important part of our lives, especially mine.

Fantasy and Festival on Ice

Backstage at the Universal Amphitheater with JoJo and Dorothy.

Hanging out with Brian Pockar.

At rehearsal with Bruno Jerry, Dorothy Hamill, and Charlie Tickner.

Emily has been through it all with us now: marriages, divorces, relationships, everything. She has been my only constant support, other than Tai. She comes out and spends weeks and weeks on end with me in Los Angeles and house-sits for me when I'm gone. When I'm in New York City, I stay with her. I know her family. She knows my family. She has really touched my life.

In 1982 Tai and I hired a personal manager, Lee Mimms. We stayed with him for two years. During that time we performed skating exhibitions whenever possible, but Lee also found us things to do outside of skating, particularly during our summers away from Ice Capades.

He signed us to do a Lee Jeans commercial. That was fun. The company constantly mailed us jeans and other merchandise.

We also did guest spots on an episode of *St. Elsewhere* for NBC. That was our first job on a major television series. It was particularly interesting for me because I had always wanted to get involved in that kind of work. We played cameo roles. Two of the lead characters went to an ice skating party, and Tai and I "happened" to be there, too. I had just a few lines.

Lee also signed us for an episode of *Hart to Hart* on ABC with Stephanie Powers and Robert Wagner. The producers hired Tai first for a fairly large role as a skating coach whose student was being menaced by the bad guy. Then they wanted me to come on board as well. We played ourselves. First we skated together. Then we shot a scene with Robert and Stephanie. Sometimes we offered suggestions to make the dialogue sound more authentic. The one thing that surprised me during that shoot was that Robert used a stand-in for his back-of-the-head closeups.

In 1984, at Tai's urging, we switched managers and signed with Michael Rosenberg. He had an interesting background in marketing for Ken and Irving Feld of Ringling Brothers and in promoting rock concerts and various musical acts. He didn't know anything about skating until Dorothy Hamill signed with him. Then he educated himself quickly about the sport and its players. He was very smart about that. Tai and

Emily Bindiger

The Great Space Coaster was a syndicated children's television show that ran from 1980 to 1987. I was one of the—pardon the expression—stars. I played the role of a sixteen-year-old named Frannie who had two male counterparts. It was puppets and us: the Mod Squad meets the Muppets. We nurtured the puppets, got them out of trouble, and taught them life's lessons. There were lots of songs and music. A big puppet named Baxter took us to exciting places on his Great Space Coaster, a spaceship styled like a roller coaster car.

Tai and Randy were booked as guest stars on our second season. I had always been a fan of theirs. I remember watching the 1980 Olympics, screaming at the television each time Randy fell. Then I saw them

in Ice Capades. When I heard that they were going to be on our show, I was just overwhelmed. The five of us met, and we all clicked. We became instant best friends. Randy and I *really* connected. He was so adorable, good-looking, and funny. I instantly fell in love with him. Our senses of humor clicked. People don't usually *get* me right away, but Randy did—totally.

Everyone fell all over Tai because she was so drop-dead gorgeous. It was like looking at a mermaid, a magical creature. We all—myself included—wanted to bend over backwards for those two beautiful people.

In that particular episode, the Great Space Coaster ended up at an ice rink, and Frannie and the boys skated with Tai and Randy. It was the first time that I'd ever been on skates and the first time that they had

I were his second skating clients. Afterward his business mushroomed. A lot of skaters signed with him because he managed us.

Michael and his wife and partner, Nancy, worked hard to keep us busy. Sometimes Tai and I boarded planes without knowing where we were going or what we were expected to do when we arrived.

"You need two numbers. Nancy will do your flights." That was our information, and we were off—not quite sure what kind of show we were booked for, not quite sure what kind of audience we would have. Usually we knew at least how much we were going to be paid.

I didn't feel pressured. Michael was just doing his job. Mind you, it is hard to say no when you are an athlete accustomed to taking orders from a coach. Still you have to be strong enough to know when to say no—when you are tired, when the show doesn't seem right for you, or when the scheduling is poor. I did say no to Michael, but not very often.

Michael took us through some of our best years as professional skaters. The three of us were a good team. He helped us, and we helped him. He signed us to Dick Button's professional skating competitions. Then, beginning in 1984, we were guest stars with Dorothy Hamill's new show, Fantasy on Ice, later called Festival on Ice.

Randy and I had the best time in Fantasy on Ice. It was a great show, and we were honored to work with Dorothy. She was a true star and still is. She and I weren't close personally, but we spent a lot of time on the ice together. When Dorothy left the show, Scott Hamilton took over as the headliner. Robin Cousins completed the last leg of the show.

Sarah Kawahara was the choreographer. She was great. Whenever you thought that you knew what she was going to do choreographically, she did just the opposite. She put together a quartet for herself, Randy, Brian Pockar, and me to the music of Ravel's

ever sung in public. We just laughed the entire time because it was so stupid. Their singing was a lot better than my skating. Let me say that I do have a beautiful pair of skates that Randy has given me, but owning them does not make me a skater. They look great once a year when I haul them out and head for Sky Rink, Wollman Rink, or Rye Playland. I'm a really good spectator, though.

Randy phoned me off and on during the year after we met. When he got his first apartment, he insisted that I go out to California to see him. I was constantly booking flights to Los Angeles. Other people were hoping that our deep friendship would turn into marriage, but we both knew better. We had a madcap platonic relationship. It was and is a real affair of the heart. I consider Randy my dearest friend, and I know that I am his.

Over the years I've made great friends through Tai and Randy: JoJo Starbuck and Ken Shelley, Scott Hamilton, Rudy Galindo, and a lot of the other skaters. I went to Vancouver to see a show that Randy choreographed for Elvis Stojko. Rudy was in that show. I don't know what clicked in him, but he figured out that he used to watch me on The Great Space Coaster. He took such delight in embarrassing me about that.

Bolero, giving each of us a different attitude to take out onto the ice. The four of us intertwined. Brian was amazing in that number.

With Dorothy we played the Universal Amphitheater in Los Angeles. It was always special when we performed at home. Our friends rarely got to see us work, so that was the time when we phoned them and got them tickets for the show. It was a big family affair. Our old friend Richard Dwyer was in the show with us. JoJo Starbuck came to visit.

It was during the early-to-mid-1980s that Tai and I began to refine our overall professional package with the help of Sarah Kawahara's choreography and Jef Billings's costumes. As soon as we were hired for a new job, we asked ourselves, "How do we want to look? What about our music and choreography?" We were concerned about having enough time to get all the details just right.

Sometimes Tai found a piece of music that she liked. Sometimes I found something. Whenever I heard music that might work for a skating number, I logged it in a journal for future reference. Sarah brought us pieces that she found on her own. Even Jef suggested things from time to time. We just threw the cassettes and records into a pile and started listening.

Sarah Kawahara

The choreographic process always begins with the music and with the question "What are we trying to say?" Sometimes the choreography comes first from the music. Sometimes the message is first. What made Tai and Randy unique was their symmetry, their ability to align their bodies. Being almost equal in height made them very linear. John Nicks in some ways fashioned them after JoJo Starbuck and Ken Shelley, but their style was quite different from Starbuck and Shelley's: more balletic, more classical. Tai and Randy both have very long arms, and that worked in their favor in achieving that sense of pendular motion.

In many ways my detailed choreographic vocabulary was contrary to Tai and Randy's movement. Maybe that's what made the collaboration exciting. I had something to offer that perhaps they didn't innately see or feel, so I could give their work those little gifts, those electrical charges.

I tried to increase their versatility over the years, venturing into different styles of music. When I met them, they were accustomed to a certain mode of classicism. I always knew that their symmetry would be their hook, but they needed to develop as people and therefore as performers. They had to test their wings a little bit and break away. In those days people weren't venturing out and breaking the mold as readily as I was pushing in that direction.

Toller Cranston and I had discussions about controversy. We agreed that sometimes it was okay to be a little bit controversial. That made you think about yourself, and it made others think about what you were thinking. When working with Tai and Randy, I really went for growth, not just parlaying what they did so well. I tried to reinvent them so that they would enjoy longevity. They were hungry to last, to have a career, not just to have a title or a tragedy kick them off into fame.

When I do a number, I always work with the costume designer. I have him come out to the rehearsal while the number is being created. Then he sees the number when it is finished. We talk about the direction of the number in the beginning and then how it has evolved once it is finished. Jef Billings was always very willing to work out the kinks in clothes. Jef, Tai, Randy, and I all grew up together in our careers.

I remember choreographing "Me and My Shadow" for Broadway on Ice, one of the Festival theater shows. I thought to myself, "Now, who's going to be the shadow?" I ended up making Tai and Randy switch back and forth. Physically they could do it, as well as from a contextual standpoint. It was fun having them take turns being the shadow.

With Sarah Kawahara and Brian Pockar in the Bolero quartet that Sarah choreographed.

The pieces didn't necessarily have to be classical, but they had to feel right for us. We knew that we weren't rap. We usually weren't rock 'n' roll either. Vocals were important to us. We could do most of the moves in Sarah's choreographic repertoire, so she felt free to go wild. Now, as we get older, she knows our limitations, but she still tries to shape us a little bit.

When it came to costumes, I liked Jef to come up with creative sketches on his own. We had so many beads and feathers in the 1980s! The look was absolutely ridiculous. Once, I had pink boa feathers coming out to *here* from my shoulders. I looked worse than Liberace, but I *loved* that costume. It was my favorite thing in the world.

Tai and I went through stages. I might say, "Jef, I'd like to be more casual this year." But I never wanted to make requests so specific that they curbed his creativity. Artists should express themselves.

In 1984 I was in a fairly good space. That was the calm between two storms. Yes, I was drinking heavily and living fast and loose, but I hadn't gone crazy yet. I was in the slow

Michael Rosenberg

Cleo Babilonia and I became friends long before Tai and I did. I met and befriended Cleo at skating events when I was the new kid in the skating world. There were four or five of us who hung around together at Nationals or Skate America. We always laughed because it was Cleo, Mary Goldblatt, Mabel Fairbanks, and I: two black women, a little Jewish lady, and a Jewish boy.

There were virtually no blacks and Jews at the top levels of skating. It seemed to me, at least, to be a Waspy sport. You could count the blacks on one hand and the Jews on two fingers: Judy Blumberg and Michael Seibert. That was it. There were very few Asians then as well.

Cleo was a gorgeous woman. I considered her the Lena Horne of the skating world. She was sweet and smart and fun to be around. Later, after I began representing Tai and Randy, I became a close friend of her husband, Connie, and of Constancio, but it all really started with Cleo and me.

As Dorothy Hamill's manager, I met Tai and Randy at various events and competitions. I admired them very much. Then one day I got a call from Randy's father. Jack came over to my office and asked, "Would you ever be interested in working with my son and Tai?"

Tai and Randy were managed by a friendly competitor of mine, Lee Mimms. I admired and liked Lee. He had been in the business longer than I had. I later became the dean of skating managers, but Lee was the dean then with Peggy Fleming, Robin Cousins, and Tai and Randy as clients.

I never talked to skaters who were under contract to another agent. I didn't solicit their business. I didn't interfere. Tai and Randy's contract with Lee Mimms was nearly up. My bottom line was "Yes, I would be interested if they parted company with Lee amicably and if it were made clear to Lee that I had never approached them to try to steal them away."

I didn't hear anything for several months. Then Mr. Gardner called me again and asked, "Would you like to meet with Tai and Randy to discuss their future?"

"Is everything fine with Lee Mimms?"

"Yes, it is."

"Good. When can we meet?"

Randy took the lead in business matters. He did more of the talking. He had much more interest than Tai in the business side. However, Tai had very strong opinions. Randy always deferred to her with sweetness and courtesy. He never said yes for both of them. Decisions were made jointly.

I love Tai and Randy as friends. Each one is complex, which made it interesting to work with them. Randy is one of a handful of my best friends. That's because of our more than fifteen years together, going through thick and thin. He is honest, sensitive, straightforward, hilarious, and smart, and he has a heart as big as he is. He is close to my daughter and Nancy. We've done many things together socially.

I trusted Randy with any and all shows that I did. He developed his choreographic, directing, and staging skills to the utmost. Whether it was the Elvis tour or buildup phase. I had lost my excess weight. My body was back in good shape, and Randy and I were both skating well. Besides, I finally understood performance.

Then, on the personal front, my life took an interesting twist.

Randy and I had a history with Peter and Kitty Carruthers that went back to the 1977 Nationals in Hartford and to the USFSA training seminars that we attended together in Squaw Valley for several weeks each summer, learning a lot and playing hard. There were dances, Ping-Pong, roller-skating, and communal living in the dorm and mess hall.

Kitty and I trained together. We dieted together. We did *everything* together. I saved every letter that she wrote to me when we were away from each other. She was very sweet and a hard worker. She gave 150 percent, even on practices, and that eventually paid off.

At some point in the late 1970s, when Randy and I performed in shows in Wilmington, Delaware, where Peter and Kitty trained, Peter and I developed a case of puppy love.

the opening of a building in Canada with a big exhibition show, I always said, "Randy will be the director and choreographer." I knew that the skaters respected him and responded to him.

I consider Tai one of the most beautiful, intelligent, sensitive, and interesting people I've ever met, with a stress on vulnerable. She looks amazing with her exotic beauty, and yet I think that she does not consider herself a beautiful woman. She has a modesty about her that is very attractive.

However, Tai kept too much inside of her. I didn't know that until later, when she started to become open after her therapy. She harbored a lot of resentment and anger toward me regarding work. My job, as I saw it, was to bring Tai and Randy every opportunity that I could. They always made the final decision. Then my job continued: protect them, get money for them, obtain the proper billing, arrange for their dressing rooms, make their travel arrangements.

I would call Tai and Randy to say, "I have such-and-such for you. What do you think?" During our three-way conversation, Randy would be all excited. *Yes, I love it. We can do it. We can work it this way. We can travel from this one to that one and still be at Dick Button's competition.* He'd be going one hundred miles an hour.

I was going just as fast. *Boy, my phone has been ringing off the hook. We're going to have a great career together.* It was no longer just Ice Capades for them, which knocks out the whole season. The free-lance deal

was going to be more interesting, more challenging, more fun, and ultimately more remunerative.

In reality it was me bringing them opportunities, Randy wanting to do it all, and Tai going along. But in Tai's mind, it became Randy and me against Tai. So naturally who was going to be resented? I was.

But Tai never showed me her feelings. Later she erupted. "You know, Michael, I have a lot of anger toward you. You just want to have us keep working. We're like a little money machine, and you keep 15 percent of the money. The more we work, the more money you make."

Of course it was totally true that I kept 15 percent of their earnings. That's what I did for a living. However, I did not pressure them to accept opportunities. Tai's memory is probably that we accepted two-thirds and turned down one-third. In truth it was more like fifty-fifty. For every good thing that came along, there was something that Tai and Randy turned down for a variety of reasons.

They were not my biggest clients. I was not dependent upon them to accept everything and make as much money as possible. Although Nancy and I got them everything from Skater of the Year to television specials to commercials to great interviews and magazine covers, in my own mind I never put pressure on them.

I hadn't begun to date yet. I was just discovering boys, and I had many innocent teenage crushes. Our particular boy-girl thing didn't last, but it was fun.

I suspect that Peter and Kitty were somewhat in awe of Randy and me in the early days. They looked up to us, just as we had looked up to JoJo and Kenny. Then they took over as American champions in 1981, after we turned professional.

In 1984, just after Peter and Kitty won their Olympic silver medals in Sarajevo, Yugoslavia, they came to the Los Angeles Forum with the Tom Collins tour. I called Peter's hotel when I got home from the show, or maybe he called me. There was some chemistry between us. A relationship started.

I was on my down time from Dorothy's show, and Peter and Kitty had just signed with Ice Capades. That summer Peter came to Los Angeles to see me. Then, when he and Kitty opened with Ice Capades in Duluth, I went to visit them on the road. That's where Peter said, "What would you do if I asked you to marry me?"

As I recall, I replied, "Ask me. I'll probably say yes."

He did and I did. It was all so quick. We were very attracted to each other. Peter bought me my engagement ring on his day off in Duluth. I went to the jewelry store with him.

"I don't want anything big," I told him. "I want something I can wear when I skate. Flat and simple."

Peter was so excited. But when we found Kitty and told her the news, she was not excited at all. I guess that she was in shock. The typical reaction from everyone I told was "Are you kidding? What are you doing? *You're* on the road. *He's* on the road."

I was happy about the engagement, because Peter and I were good friends. I did fear that it was too soon for both of them. I also worried that Tai would lose her focus on our career, which was *my* thing at the time. Anyone whose livelihood is dependent upon a partner feels vulnerable.

I attempted to be a big brother to Tai, but I wasn't as verbal then as I try to be now. I tended to accept her choices on the surface while keeping my feelings and opinions to myself. When Peter asked me to be his best man, I gladly agreed. I didn't see real trouble coming. Not at all.

Peter and I were not ready for marriage. We didn't act like a couple about to tie the knot. I don't believe that we even set a date. That just wasn't realistic. We talked about getting a house and settling down, but we didn't know what we were doing. We were too young. We both traveled too much. Our adult lives had just started—his even more than mine.

Then Peter and I began fighting. To be honest, I was a little envious of Peter and Kitty as skaters. At the time, Randy and I weren't working as much as they were.

With Dorothy.

We weren't getting the specials and endorsements that they were getting. They were the hot pair of the moment, and rightly so. I had a hard time with that. I felt threatened.

I remember us being apart from one another, talking on the phone. There was game playing—mostly on my part because I wasn't taking the engagement seriously. Kitty picked up on that. She knew that the relationship wasn't going to work. Women just know those things.

The situation came to a head during the 1984 World Professional Figure Skating Championships in Landover, Maryland. The four of us were competing head to head. On the night before the event, Peter and I had a fight, and I locked him out of my hotel room. I told him, "I can't do this, Peter. I have to be alone. I have to compete tomorrow." The situation was ugly. That was when I knew the truth. *This can't work. I won't even let him into my room, and we're engaged? Hello!* I was clueless.

The next day we were both tired. I felt anxious, so I took a few drinks backstage in a bathroom stall before competing. Straight from the bottle. I had a big purse and a little flask. I didn't drink a lot. Just enough to feel nice and relaxed.

Randy and I skated well. However, Barbara Underhill and Paul Martini won the event. Ludmila and Oleg Protopopov finished second. Peter and Kitty were third, followed by Randy and me. That was where my relationship with Peter ended.

Several years after our breakup, Peter married Dena, a chorus skater from Ice Capades. She is wonderful. They are a perfect couple.

Peter and I are only now getting comfortable with one another. He is a figure skating commentator, and he is very good at his job. When we ran into each other once on tour, I said, "Peter, I'm so proud of you. You have found your niche," and he has. It helps that we are both parents now. That makes all the youthful angst seem so silly. But our romance was a part of growing up, and I wouldn't change it for anything.

At the midpoint of the 1980s, serious trouble was brewing, but I managed to hide it from others for a long time. I was good at hiding things, good at faking it. Some things I even hid from myself. The problems with substance abuse that started while I toured with Ice Capades still had a few years to run. Drinking made the strains of life on the road tolerable. It helped me to suppress bad memories, past traumas, unresolved issues, and frustrations. There is a lot that I don't remember from that period.

Off the ice, away from Randy, I maintained a wild lifestyle. I ended up in places where I should not have been, at parties that I should not have attended—everywhere, all over Los Angeles. I was burning myself out.

I met so many people. It was the 1980s, and I guess that I felt free. Clothes were wild then. I had the big mall hair, the nails, and the boots. I befriended the members of a number of rock groups and hung out with them backstage at their concerts. That existence made quite a contrast to the narrow, perfectly disciplined, obedient life that I had led as a competitive skater. I had fun—very risky fun at times.

Mall hair in a 1987 publicity shot.

People who knew me then will approach me now at parties and ask, "Do you remember me?" That is extremely embarrassing. *I didn't do that. That wasn't me.* I could kick myself now. How could I have let myself get so wacky?

Randy and I worked non-stop during those years: at Knott's Berry Farm, in many of the Festival shows, at Bally's, in Disney and Crystal Gale television specials.

In December 1985 Randy and I finally won at Landover, skating to music from the film *On Golden Pond*. That was our last year at Dick Button's World Professional Championships. We beat Underhill and Martini and Peter and Kitty, and we tied the Protopopovs for first place. What an honor! The Protopopovs were legends. We had worked with them when they came in to do guest spots in Ice Capades, and they were very kind and pleasant to us. Oleg was a character and a skating purist. His whole life was skating. Both he and Ludmila were dedicated, encouraging, and inspirational to be with.

Landover was more fun in the early days when it was a team event and a big reunion. I always looked forward to seeing Kenny and JoJo, the Bezics, and Janet Lynn. By the mid-1980s the competition had become very serious. It was high-energy. There was always a packed house. The money had gotten bigger, and some of the fun had gone out of the event.

Five years after the Olympics, Tai and I still had a fairly high public profile. Our fans were wonderful, but occasionally someone overstepped the boundaries of good taste and common sense. During Ice Capades someone had posted nasty pictures on Tai's trunk. That was more offensive yet less troubling than the very nice young teenaged girl who frequently wrote to me, three or four handwritten pages at a time, on school notebook paper. All of a sudden she wanted Tai and me to become her parents. She asked us in so many words, "Would you be my mom and dad?" It was sad. What could we do?

Then there were the two sisters in the Washington, D.C., area—nice girls but, boy, were they vigilant! They wrote letters and sent chocolates. When we performed nearby, they wanted to stand backstage, watch me walk in and leave, and give me something in person. That was fine. After our Ice Capades days ended, Tai and I stopped skating at their local arena. I didn't hear much from them for six or seven years. Then we played Bally's in Atlantic City, and there they were in the coffee shop! I sent dessert to their table and waved to them. Later they came to see the show.

By the mid-1980s I had purchased a condominium in Marina del Rey, in a corner building not far from the ocean. That was where my only really scary fan episode occurred. One day my neighbor told me, "Randy, I was talking to some people who were parked out here next to the building, and when you pulled out of your parking space in the garage, they suddenly said, 'There he is. We've got to go.'"

My neighbor jumped to the conclusion that I was being investigated for some reason. I assured him, "Mike, I didn't do *anything*."

Off and on for many weeks a black Nissan 240Z, a two-seater sports car, arrived outside my condominium and parked by the curb. There were two people in the car, a man and a woman, probably in their thirties. They varied their appearance by wearing minor disguises like hats and wigs. When I drove away, they followed me. As a result, every time I drove away from my condominium, I looked to see if anyone was on my tail. Occasionally the same couple showed up in a different car.

Sometimes I felt as though they *were* investigating me, and I wondered what I could have done wrong. At other times I just felt as though I was in the middle of an episode of *Murder, She Wrote*. Once, I was driving up into Hollywood on the freeway when I noticed the couple following me. I got off at the next exit and pretended that I was about to make a left-hand turn. I turned on my blinker and got into the left-hand pocket. As soon as the light was about to change to red, I took off straight ahead and left them behind.

Another time, as I drove down the Marina del Rey peninsula with the couple in pursuit, I turned into the driveway of a large apartment complex and zigzagged through the rows of cars. I kind of enjoyed watching the couple's reactions. At one point we came face to face. I wrote down their license plate number and held up the paper and pencil to make sure that they knew what I was doing.

In 1985 we finally won the World Professional Figure Skating Championships at Landover.

Rehearsing for Liberty Weekend at the Meadowlands with Dorothy Hamill and producer Don Ohlmeyer.

Then I called Tai's dad, Connie, who still worked for the LAPD. He traced the plates and learned the identity of the previous owner, an older man who clearly had nothing to do with the people who were stalking me. The car had recently changed hands, and the transaction hadn't yet been documented. My pursuers didn't know that, however, and that was the last that I saw of them.

As we plowed through the second half of the 1980s, Randy and I continued to be busier than I liked to be. In addition to performing often, in 1987 we made an instructional home video, *How to Ice Skate*, the first of its kind, produced by Michael Rosenberg. Randy and I co-wrote and hosted the show. We directed the information toward beginners: how to choose and lace skates, first steps on the ice, stroking, the role of the USFSA, and that kind of thing. We filmed the video at the North Hollywood rink. John Nicks even appeared in a scene, and his young skaters participated in our demonstrations.

Randy and I were always doing *something*. I remember being on planes a lot and saying yes to every offer. "Strike while the iron is hot," I told myself. "A skating career doesn't last forever."

Randy loved it all. He skated well. He looked great. He had fun. When he said yes, I really had no choice. I didn't want to seem like a big baby. I said yes because I felt that I had to, even if I was dead tired.

I didn't understand much about emotions, about unhappiness. I have never understood where deep unhappiness comes from. I was always on a fairly even keel, just going along with my life. I did things, handled things, and fulfilled my obligations.

Tai began acting a little strange. She didn't seem unhappy to me, but she was scattered. She made snap decisions. Sometimes she didn't show up for rehearsals. Fortunately she always managed to arrive for our skating performances.

We were supposed to participate in a celebrity fashion show for the Amanda Foundation, an animal rescue organization. Tai didn't phone to make her excuses. She simply didn't show up. Even her mother didn't know where she was, so I walked down the runway by myself.

Tai was all over the board emotionally in those days. The pattern began while we were with Ice Capades, but I didn't really notice it until later, during Festival on Ice, when the situation reached a full boil.

I knew that Tai was partying. I just assumed that she was having a good time. I observed her drinking, but I didn't see her drinking heavily. I didn't realize the extent to which she was hiding some of the drinking. When she told me that she didn't want to do this job or that job, I convinced myself that her reservations weren't serious. *Oh well, maybe she's tired right now. She's just having a bad day.* I viewed her from my own frame of reference.

Tai unloaded on me in dribs and drabs. One day when we were at a rehearsal site in Las Vegas, she needed to take a rest. We sat down next to one another. Suddenly she blurted out, "You know, I am aware that you and Michael Rosenberg talk about me all the time." I had no idea where that remark came from. Michael and I did not make a practice of talking about Tai behind her back. But everything was magnified for her in those days. Her feelings were right on the surface. Every little scenario became intense, emotional, and vivid in her mind.

There was a period in 1987 when I sold my condo in Sherman Oaks—I don't know why—and moved into a hotel, the Chateau Marmont on Sunset Boulevard. The memories are all rather blurry. I didn't have time to find another place to buy, and I didn't want to live with my parents, so I put my belongings in storage and checked into the hotel for two months.

Randy and I worked constantly and made very good money, probably the most money that we ever made during our career. We signed lucrative contracts, but I was a mess. I was fed up with it all. My life was just work, work, work, work, work. There wasn't time to relish the atmosphere. Maybe I should have lounged by the pool and read a book, but I didn't do that. Now I would.

I was in such a space there. We did an interview at the Dorothy Chandler Pavilion in 1987, while I was living at the Chateau Marmont. I was miserable, absolutely out of it, and the photographer captured that. It was a sad day.

Tai's Lost Decade

We appeared in the Caesars Palace Christmas show in Las Vegas. Then we skated in the Festival on Ice Christmas show with Robin Cousins at the Dorothy Chandler Pavilion. I was not in good shape. I was not there mentally. Randy and I were performing so many different routines that I had trouble remembering them all. The drinking didn't help my powers of recall. I was in a downward spiral, getting little or no sleep. That was the beginning of the end of life as I once knew it.

When we finished the two Christmas runs, we were exhausted. Still we continued skating. The next week we moved on to Festival on Ice at Harrah's in Lake Tahoe with Scott Hamilton. The situation quickly reached a climax. By then my alcohol intake was heavy. There was a lot of junk in my system. I threw things and lost my temper easily.

At Harrah's Randy and I shared the stars' huge dressing room suite. It included a large pink bathroom and a sitting room with couches, chairs, and a bar. After all, we were playing a showroom. When Sammy Davis came in the next week, he would use the same dressing room. That's just how it was in those days.

I had the habit of sneaking a drink before a performance. I would arrive a little early and have some brandy, and I actually was able to skate that way. That ability may have had something to do with my rigorous early training and long years of performing.

Scott Hamilton

Tai and I were good friends for a long time, and then I started Stars on Ice and went my own way. We were all very active, very busy, but in separate parts of the country. It wasn't until recently that Tai and I started to become close friends again after a rough spot in our relationship.

I performed with Tai and Randy at Harrah's for two years in a row. The way I remember it, during the second year Tai didn't show up for rehearsals for a few days. Then, when she did show up, she wasn't happy at all. She was in a bad way.

Tai and I weren't getting along then at all, and I didn't know whether or not she was unhappy with *me*. It was weird. I had always been one of Tai and Randy's friends. In many respects I was a wannabe. Then I came into my own. Where did I fit in a show that they had established? Was I a guest? Was I a star?

I didn't know what was going on in Tai's private life. You know what your comrades are capable of doing once you all get to the building, but many times, even though skating is a very small community, people do their own things and go their own ways.

From my perspective, the strain between Tai and me had nothing to do with her breakup with Peter Carruthers, although that had certainly been an unfortunate incident. Pete and I were really good friends. Kitty and I had dated for many years. Our romance was kind of a soap opera. Then the first time that Peter, Kitty,

Tai, and Randy competed against each other as pros was the moment Tai chose to break off the engagement. Pete and I had been touring together and competing in the same places for four years, so I was more current with him than I was with Tai. He needed a shoulder, and I was there for him.

Nothing against Tai. It's tough when two people are in the same business but they're never going to tour together. That's not an easy way to start a relationship. Everybody, even now, has a lot of growing up to do. Competitive skaters are in an unreal world forever. How can we deal with the pressures and the demands?

If Tai and Randy didn't talk about the Olympics afterward, sometimes those things can become toxic. Maybe that's what happened with Tai at Harrah's. Randy is so laid back. People who know him realize that nothing flusters him. Nothing gets him agitated, aggravated, upset, or irate. He just rolls with it. However, you don't really know where he stands on certain issues. Tai is more emotional. You *know* where she stands.

That difference could have been a part of what went on between them in Lake Tahoe. They had never really cleared the air. You can run, but you can't hide. Things like the Olympic episode need to be discussed. They need to be figured out if you are going to be able to look back on that period of your life with any level of closure or satisfaction.

Whatever the reasons, I consistently got through my numbers standing up. However, I would not like to see those videotapes today.

One night I was a little loopy. While Randy and I were performing our routine, I fell —but I didn't get right back up. I just started laughing. In the main showroom at Harrah's! It was the dinner performance. (There were two shows nightly, dinner and cocktail.) I eventually picked myself up, left the ice, and went backstage to the dressing room. Sarah Kawahara came storming in.

"What is wrong? What is the problem? Don't make a fool of yourself. Don't make a joke of this show that I choreographed."

Randy and I were scheduled to tour after the Harrah's engagement. I was determined not to do that tour. I was determined to end it all at Harrah's: either to take a break from skating or to quit altogether.

It was a night or two later when Randy insisted, "No, you can't quit. You are doing the tour. You signed a contract."

I didn't want to hear those words. That was when I snapped and had a nervous breakdown. I swung as hard as I could and hit Randy. I pushed him. I threw things. I ended up under the counter in the big, pink bathroom, crying hysterically and saying between sobs, "I can't do it. I'm so tired."

Randy told me later that I looked like a Tasmanian devil, flailing, hitting, screaming, and crying. He was in shock. I certainly had never hit him before.

I didn't expect what happened. Tai was sitting there putting her makeup on for the second show, informing me that she didn't want to continue on with the tour. I told her, "Well, you know that you have to do it."

"I'm not doing it."

"Yes, you are."

Emily Bindiger

I became engaged in New York on Valentine's Day 1988 during the Olympic pairs event. (The wedding never took place. It's just as well.) I remember very specifically watching Gordeeva and Grinkov win their gold medal in Calgary that night. Just a few days later I went to Lake Tahoe to hang out with Randy and Tai. Something was clearly up.

I was sitting in the anteroom of their dressing room one evening, watching the Olympic ladies' event on television, when Tai stormed in. She went into the back part of the dressing room complex, to the place where they put on their makeup, and Randy followed her.

There was a commotion. Tai began hitting Randy. When Randy came out, stone faced, he said, "Em, let's turn off the TV, okay? I think that there's been enough skating." I left at that point and hung out with Scott Hamilton.

Months later Tai wrote to me and apologized for her bad behavior. I thought, "What are you apologizing for? You were in a lot of pain." Looking back, I think that we all should have seen some of the signs of distress. Tai refused to eat. She kept to herself a lot. Maybe we shouldn't have let her, but she was very private. She still is.

"I'm not. Watch this. I'll leave now."

She threw down her eyebrow pencil and stood up to leave. I went to stop her, and the physical confrontation began. Only then did I realize that Tai's problem was serious. She scared me. I had never been in a position like that before.

As far as I knew, though, Tai simply didn't want to work as much as I did. I still didn't understand the depth and meaning of it all.

Somehow I got back onto the ice and did the second show that evening. The picture in my mind is a little fuzzy. I did complete the run at Harrah's, and I managed to do the tour afterward, but I insisted on my brother going with me. I just had to have something or someone to hold onto. I begged Constancio. I pleaded, "I'll pay you anything. Just be there."

Constancio came through for me. Throughout the tour he was there when I got on the ice, and he was there when I got off. *Just get her through it!* He did. I thank him for that.

In February I couldn't even watch Brian Boitano win his Olympic gold medal. Brian was much younger than Randy and I, but we had always encountered him at Pacific Coasts and thought that he had a lot of talent. He was athletic and fast, even when he was just a little guy. Right after we turned pro, Randy sent a check to the USFSA Memorial Fund to support Brian's skating. But when Brian grew up and made it to the 1988 Olympics, I was too disaffected from the sport to watch him compete. Whenever someone turned on the skating competition on the huge television set in our dressing room, I turned it right off. Eventually I saw Brian's great performance on tape.

After the tour ended, I made a declaration. "Okay, I'm retiring. I did this tour. Now I'm done. I have to find some kind of balance in my life. I have to do something else. This is driving me nuts."

My announcement hit the papers. Our manager, Michael Rosenberg, acknowledged the finality of my decision. "Okay, Tai. You have quit."

Sarah Kawahara

I knew that there was something wrong. Tai was reclusive. Her moods were erratic. Tai and Randy's temperament with each other, however, continued to be neutral. I always thought that was a little odd. They both had protective outer shells. They weren't sure how much to expose of their inner selves. Part of that was choice. Part of that was maturity level. It's part of the human psyche, and I'd rather not judge them for it. I just know that, because of that reticence, Tai's problems were compounded. She was in trouble but didn't know how to communicate.

Tai left the ice once in the middle of a number, and Randy followed her. I went backstage, and I was mad.

Performers don't leave the stage. I didn't care what the problem was. Their behavior was unprofessional. They were headliners of a distinguished show. The audience was great. The Harrah's people were really good to us, and to Tai and Randy in particular.

Tai and Randy knew that what they had done was wrong, but the damage was done. When I confronted them, suddenly they confronted each other with retorts. That was healthy, I thought. If the incident had made them respond spontaneously to each other, then it wasn't all for naught. It was maybe a day later when Tai had her breakdown.

The problem was that I didn't want to quit. I was crying for help. I was physically and mentally exhausted. With everything that I was doing to abuse my system, with every substance that I was ingesting, I was a mess.

Randy thought that I would never really quit skating, which was something that I didn't want to hear at that moment.

When he told me, "Nah, you're not quitting," I replied, "Watch me!"

I considered throwing my skates into a trashcan at my Los Angeles apartment building. *No, somebody will find them there. I don't want anyone to find them and return them to me, because I won't wear them anymore.* That's how I reasoned.

So I drove to Santa Barbara, something that I liked to do once in a while. In the television movie *On Thin Ice*, the actress who played me took a long walk to the end of the pier—it was beautiful—and flung her skates, slow motion, into the Pacific Ocean. In real life I tossed them into a gutter. I parked my car next to a Santa Barbara gutter and sat on the hood holding those instruments of torture.

"Goodbye, skates."

I let them go. Then I heard a clunk. That's the state of mind I was in. I was done with skating.

I felt relieved, scared, sad, and confused—all at the same time. More than anything, I felt confused. *What will I do if I don't skate? I don't do anything else.*

I drove home to my apartment feeling miserable. I stopped answering the phone. My answering machine filled up with messages.

I was determined to find an alternative to skating. *Well, I'll just get a regular job like a regular person.* I started talking to people about my prospects. They must have thought that I was absolutely crazy. I even went to a local mall and investigated the possibility of selling jewelry. I just wanted to feel what it would be like to be normal. I craved normality in my life. That was why I had brought my brother on the road.

In June, although I was terrified, I decided to attend Alcoholics Anonymous meetings to clean up my act. What were people going to think when they recognized me? *I've seen that figure skater on television. What is she doing here?*

The group met in various locations throughout the area. Sometimes the gathering was large. I found it intimidating to have to stand up and talk about my difficulties with so many strangers surrounding me and listening.

Tai and I agreed that she would take a personal leave for as long as it took her to work through her problems. Whether or not we would ever skate together again was questionable at that point. I had a lot of time to think about how my fate was tied to hers. If her career was over, mine was, too. That was when I decided to try choreography.

I had often worked with Sarah Kawahara, a Canadian genius who choreographed most of our numbers from 1985 on. I mentioned to her that I would like to begin doing some choreography of my own. She happened to need an assistant for the 1988 Sea World summer ice show in San Diego. That was my first break. Sarah choreographed the show and left me to run it for her all summer. I learned about managing people and keeping a show intact.

Theme park presentations are great shows to train on. Besides having generous rehearsal time available, you work with the park management and learn about the administrative end of putting shows together. It is not just a question of choreography. Politics are involved as well. I learned that early on.

I rented an apartment in San Diego and drove home to my condo in Marina del Rey on my days off. I commuted daily if I could swing it. There were many Los Angeles-area skaters in the show, so we caravaned or carpooled. Several times I even brought along my cat, Emi, to make the San Diego apartment seem more homelike.

While, by necessity, I was planning and building a career without Tai, I went to check in on her from time to time.

I managed to stay sober for sixty-nine days. Then, in September of 1988, I fell off the wagon and began to carry on a destructive interior monologue. *Okay, I have no reason to be here on earth. Everyone is mad at me because I quit skating. I'm miserable, and I'm not doing anyone any good. Here's a way to go see Jimi Hendrix. Finally I can meet him up in heaven.* That is how out of it I was.

I drove deep into the Valley looking for a drugstore where no one knew me. I bought some sleeping pills. I also purchased a ring. I don't know why. I just wanted to buy something.

When I got home, I wrote a will. I explained, "Everyone around me is so unhappy, and I don't want that. It would be much better if I just left." Then I cleaned the apartment and fed my cat.

A Poem by Tai

wings

relax and enjoy
    I find it hard to do
consumed with addictions
    only few knew
a loss of control
    confused and scared
afraid to reach out
    to those who had cared
i'll say goodbye
    without a sound
wings worn as a child
    nowhere to be found

The sleeping pills weren't in a bottle. They came in packets that had to be opened individually. I tore open all the packets, picked up the handful of pills, and washed them down with alcohol. Then I lay down on my bed.

Instead of falling asleep, I started to sweat. "Just sleep, just sleep," I told myself repeatedly. Maybe subconsciously I was fighting for my life by keeping myself awake. Looking back, I recognize that the suicide attempt was a cry for help.

I became incredibly sick to my stomach. The room started spinning. I must have been somewhat lucid, because I was able to dial my mother's number on the phone next to my bed. After that I don't remember anything except ending up on the floor near the front door. My father and an ambulance arrived at the same time. The rescue team broke down the door. Then the paramedics put me on a stretcher.

I don't remember being lifted into the ambulance. Nor do I remember the ride to Cedars-Sinai Hospital. However, I do definitely remember getting my stomach pumped. That was when the light in my head went on. I don't wish a stomach pumping experience upon anyone. It was horrible. Randy showed up while the medical team was still working on me.

Tai's mother had called Michael Rosenberg. I was at home at around nine o'clock on the morning of September 14 when Michael phoned and told me, "Go to the hospital. They're taking Tai to Cedars-Sinai."

I already knew at that point that Tai wasn't going to die. The doctors had said that she was going to make it. Still, I was concerned and scared. I'll admit that anger was part of my reaction, too. My career was on the line. *Brother! Was it an attention-getter? What was it?* I couldn't understand why Tai had done something so drastic. I still don't know.

Michael Rosenberg

I didn't realize that there was trouble until Harrah's. Of course I knew that Tai was not as excited about their career as Randy was. I knew that Tai had a weight problem and that she wasn't enthusiastic about keeping herself in perfect shape. People who bought the act brought that to my attention.

The promoters would call me later, at my request. "Oh, Tai and Randy were wonderful. They were very cooperative." Every once in a while I'd get a candid response. "They were very good, very professional to work with. Tai, as you know, is a little heavy. She looked a little chubby out there."

When Tai and Randy came back from a job, I called Randy to see how it had gone. "It went great!" As soon as I hung up, I called Tai. How did it go? "Oh, it was all right." In that regard I sensed that there were some problems, that Tai was not a happy camper. She was professional, but she was not enjoying her career. That was a sign, but it wasn't the kind of sign that would alert

me to think, "Uh oh, I have a girl who potentially could commit suicide, or a girl who is in the closet secretly drinking."

Tai and Randy's big fight in the dressing room at Harrah's was a total shock to Randy and me. We both thought, "Oh, my God!"

I didn't witness the slugfest. Randy told me about it afterward. Then I went into shock. I felt horrible. One of the very distasteful things that I had to do, from a business point of view, was to tell Tai and Randy, "If you breach the contract that is already signed, sealed, and advertised without good reason, then you will be sued —at least for the recovery of all costs that the promoter has incurred and for any potential income that he might have realized. Or else we have to lie and say that you are injured." It was my job to paint the picture for them.

After a number of days or maybe even a week, Tai said, "Okay, I'll do it." At least we were off the hook

Tai's Lost Decade

That kind of choice is not in my psyche.

Cleo Babilonia was there when I arrived at the hospital. She was calm by then, just happy and relieved that Tai was alive.

Some parents and friends spend a lot of time in denial. I don't think that any of us—Cleo and Connie, my parents, or me—had understood until that moment the depth of Tai's emotional distress. Maybe we had all simply dismissed the situation as temporary. Nobody wants to deal with that kind of crisis. Nobody wants to acknowledge that it is real.

Everyone finally understood. *There is something wrong with this girl. First of all, she does have to stop. She can't skate right now. She needs help. She needs a break.*

After the medical team finished pumping my stomach, the hospital assigned me a psychotherapist for follow-up care. When I headed home, there were paparazzi outside the hospital and at my apartment door. It is strange how quickly media organizations learn bad news.

I remember my stomach really hurting after I got home. I felt very tired. I also felt embarrassed about what I had done. When you consider suicide, you don't realize that you are going to hurt anyone else. I believed that I was going to make everything all better by not being around anymore. The fact that I had reached that point is pretty scary.

My mother stayed with me for a few nights. She was understandably worried.

I was required to go to the therapist three times a week. I hated that. I hated getting up in the morning and going to talk about my problems. I didn't think that I needed

for potential lawsuits. But boy, was it scary until then. Randy was beside himself. He was worried not only about the immediate future but about the long-term future as well, and so was I.

On September 14, Cleo called me and said, "Tai has attempted suicide. She's at Cedars-Sinai." Nancy and I just stopped everything. We were horrified. Within twenty minutes I received the first calls from the press.

When I talked to Randy, he and I agreed that since he was going to the hospital, Nancy and I would stay in our office and handle all the calls that were flooding in. But how were we going to handle them? Did we try to cover up the truth? Did we tell the whole story? We were thinking on our feet.

I believe that for the first hour or two, we said that Tai had taken an accidental overdose of a prescription drug. We were trying to protect her to the *n*th degree, thinking that we could get away with it. First, she was alive. Second, who could ever dispute whether it had

been a suicide attempt or an accident?

Two, three, or maybe four hours later, after Nancy and I talked to Randy, it became clear to us that the truth would come out regardless. Somebody at the hospital had told the press that Tai had attempted suicide. That was the end of that. Then all we could do was spin the truth in the most protective way possible.

Tai's career was apparently over, but none of us—Cleo, Connie, Randy, Nancy, me—cared about that. We only cared that Tai was going to be okay. That's the truth. At that point we all said, "Who cares about money? Who cares about fame? We care about Tai's life and health."

to. In those days I didn't truly know what therapy was. *Who are you? I don't know you. Why should I tell you anything?*

I did need the therapy, though, and I learned to love it. Eventually I opened up. It was a slow process. I came to love going back to when I was a child, slowly piecing together where my problems began and how they impacted my adult life. Then everything made sense.

Yes, the Olympics were festering. No one, including Randy, had ever really talked about them with me, and I had just tucked them away in a psychological cupboard the way everyone else had. Finally I couldn't tuck anything away anymore. The cupboard was full.

But the identity issue was a bigger part of my problem. Having my identity submerged in Tai and Randy scared me to death, especially when I announced that I planned to quit skating. I was scared because I believed that I had nothing to fall back on. (I actually did have resources, but I hadn't tapped into them yet.) I didn't know whether or not I could function on my own, and I didn't know who I was apart from Randy.

I have always loved being a part of Tai and Randy. You see, I can put that in its place. I can put my personal life in its place. I can put my individual career in its place. There are different categories. I am all of those things. Those are the things that make *me*. Perhaps I have more confidence than Tai, but there are gender differences, too. Being part of the Tai and Randy identity was a different experience for her because she is a woman.

I admire female executives and female Ironman triathletes, but there is no denying that males and females, in general, are different from each other both emotionally and

JoJo Starbuck

Kenny and I were such fans of Tai and Randy. We felt like their family, watching them win their world title. We were there at the Olympics, too. That was heartbreaking.

After the pairs event was over, I spent time at the house Tai's parents had rented, but we didn't talk about what had happened. Tai and Randy had a way of putting on bright and sunny faces and not letting their emotions show, which was astounding to me in light of what had just happened. I don't know who trained them to do that. Maybe Mr. Nicks did. I am so emotional. I was amazed at how stoic they could be. I had thought, "We need to help them through this trauma," but they carried on as though it was no big deal.

Obviously what was going on inside unveiled itself later in a most unpleasant way when Tai had her problems. I guess Randy had other ways of escaping and dealing with everything. I admired his manner. *Okay. It's another day at the office. I can handle it.* You never saw him break down, as I would have if the same thing had happened to me. I think that Randy and Kenny are similar in that they don't want to show their emotions to the world. They are very private people. Everything is always fine. Certain unspoken boundaries are there.

But when push comes to shove, I know that Kenny would do anything for me, and I certainly would do anything for him. I think that it is the same with Tai and Randy. In a way, the nature of the relationship is almost too precious to verbalize. It is so tender and emotional, and the experiences are so rich—both the highs and the lows—that you can hardly say how you feel and what you mean to each other.

physically. I understand Tai's feelings now. Her whole identity was wrapped up in our partnership.

While Tai grappled with those issues, I got my new choreographic career off the ground. I was hired to do a show of my own, the Knott's Berry Farm Christmas show, Holiday Festival on Ice. Then I made my début as a solo skating act on January 18, 1989, when Festival on Ice played the McCallum Theatre for the Performing Arts at the Bob Hope Cultural Center in Palm Desert.

I enrolled at an art school, the Otis Parsons School of Design in downtown Los Angeles, just to see what that was like and to catch the bug again by being around artists. In delving into my creativity, I tried to find a balance in my life. I started with sketching, then took a jewelry-making class. Eventually I came to create and sell my own line of butterfly jewelry and hair ornaments. (I still do.) Finally I was able to realize that I didn't have to *just skate*. I could do other things. I hadn't known that I could.

My suicide attempt made people listen. It opened everyone's eyes and got them to take me seriously. It opened my eyes, too, and it taught me to open my mouth. If you don't want to do something, just say no. I had never known how to do that. I learned to say no during those months away from the ice. I also spent a lot of time returning phone calls, assuring everyone that I was okay.

One day in February or March of 1989 I returned to the ice on my own. I went to the rink casually dressed with a baseball cap on my head. I didn't want anyone to know who I was. I was paranoid. Then I gave myself a pep talk. "Just get the feel of it. Just start to find the love for skating that you had as a child." That love had gotten lost along the way.

I expect that every skater goes through some loss of the sheer joy of the sport. It is so easy to get caught up in the work and the money. I wanted to feel the ice again. *Just float. Just stroke. Just glide.* That is exactly what I did. It was part of the healing process.

Another part of the healing process was giving an interview to *People* magazine for the April 17 issue. I thought that it would be the perfect outlet for the story of my nervous breakdown and suicide attempt. I wanted to get it all out, to stop lying to people and start over. *Okay. Now they all know.* Many skaters weren't happy about my decision. I believe that they laughed at the article because they didn't know how serious the situation had been or how desperately I needed to tell the story. Some viewed the article as a publicity stunt. My parents were okay with it. They didn't *love* it, but then I didn't do it for them. It was for me, and it was perfect.

Randy had been skating solo, touring in Broadway on Ice with the same cast that had performed in the Festival shows. The time came for me to phone him. *Okay, I'm ready.* Then we got a call from Michael Rosenberg about a job in Celebration on Ice at Bally's in Atlantic City with Brian Pockar and Lisa-Marie Allen. That was the ideal vehicle for a new start. Randy and I opened on June 14, 1989, exactly nine months to the day after my suicide attempt.

I was petrified in Atlantic City because I didn't know what people were thinking while I was onstage. *Oh, God, is she still a mess? Or is she okay?* But it was great. I was ready. I was in fairly good shape. My therapist went along on the road with me.

Granted, I was nervous because it was a big challenge to get back out there on the ice. The first few shows were fine. Everything went well. Then one night a lift went down wrong. Randy didn't exactly drop me, but I ended up hitting the ice chin first, and the skin split. I left crying. Then I went to the hospital and got myself stitched up. For a few days I skated with a bandage on my chin. My confidence slipped, but somehow I was able to build it back up.

I am sure that Randy and I lost some work because of my history. Once you try something like suicide, for the rest of your life people look at you differently. That act is pretty heavy. Some promoters may not have wanted to take a chance on me. They were afraid that I would slip back into the old Tai.

While Tai was getting her life back together, tragedy touched my family. My father had been struggling with emphysema and heart disease. Doctors discussed sending him to Texas for surgery, but they weren't confident that he could survive the stress of the flight and the open-heart procedure. He was up and around, though. He had quit smoking, and he took heart medication.

One Saturday morning at the end of October 1989, Mom, Dad, and Gordy were planning to go to a football game together. At eight-thirty or nine, my mother called for my father, but he didn't answer. She went downstairs, found him on the kitchen floor, and called 911. I was at my condominium taking a shower when I received her phone call.

By the time I arrived, the ambulance had taken Dad to the hospital. I drove to the emergency room, but he was already gone. I think that he had died in the kitchen despite the heroic attempts to revive him.

I regret not being closer to my dad before he died. It's the familiar cliché about should haves, could haves, and would haves. I wish that I had told him more often that I loved him. I wish that I had involved him more in my life on a personal level. I suggest that people do that while their parents are still alive.

Robin Cousins

I knew Tai during the rough years, but I didn't know that they were rough. When we toured Florida with Festival on Ice, the three of us had a limousine that took us from town to town. I hope that I knew Tai well enough that if I had thought something was up, I would have talked to her about it. Randy certainly never let on that anything was wrong, and Tai concealed whatever she was concealing so well.

There was a chunk of time when I wasn't involved with any of the old gang. We were doing our own things. It was really sad to hear about Tai's problems. Then she got into her angel era and her butterflies, off in the clouds as she was, but there are all sorts of philosophical and psychological reasons behind the things that we do.

Tai's Lost Decade

Losing my father changed our family forever. Instead of four, we were three. You really feel that shift when there's a person missing. Those of us who remained experienced a change in the family dynamics. Fortunately we grew closer together.

The next month Tai and I were reminded again of the impermanence of life when we performed at an AIDS benefit, "Skating for Life: A Celebration of Champions," at the New York State Armory in New York City.

Meanwhile some people at Spectacor Films who had seen the *People* article contacted Michael Rosenberg about making a television movie, *On Thin Ice: The Tai Babilonia Story*. I said, "Great!" I wasn't working at the time. Once again I had found the perfect outlet—or it had found me.

The producers hired Randy and me as consultants. Randy also choreographed the skating sequences, and he did a great job. That was a stepping stone for him. He got his feet wet in film.

A writer came to work with me and with the other sources in the Los Angeles area. He spent about two weeks gathering information. I didn't go into every sordid detail with him, but I told him what he needed to know to write the script. Then I made some changes, gave my approval, and went off to shoot the film in Toronto for a month and a half during the late fall. I was so miserable during the first week of shooting that I wanted to return home immediately.

There were three different Tais in the movie: the eight-year-old, the twelve-year-old, and the teenager. A Canadian actress, Rachael Crawford, played me as a teenager, and she did it well. Charlie Stratton played Randy. Both actors had to quickly learn how to skate. Randy and I worked with them between shots. That part was fun. The hard part was watching the taking of the pills, the ambulance scene, and the portrayal of my mother panicking. Those memories were too fresh and painful.

Denise Nicholas from *Room 222* played the role of my mother. William Daniels from *St. Elsewhere* played Mr. Nicks. Without ever meeting John Nicks, William captured him perfectly.

Certain incidents are often purposely overdramatized in a film based on a true story. That happened in *On Thin Ice*. I had overall control of the project, but some things I had to let go—like the inaccurate skate-throwing scene.

I was glad to be a part of making the film, trying to get things done as authentically as possible. As it turned out, some of the situations, some of the environments that the filmmakers put us in—especially the competition scenes—didn't look authentic. Some incidents were overdramatized. Other incidents weren't treated in sufficient depth. It's not that the filmmakers distorted the overall reality. Their key points were fine. Although they changed certain names and episodes, psychologically they cut pretty close to the truth.

Tai and I helped with the writing and did a lot of doubling for the actors when they skated. All the actors' portrayals were fine. I enjoyed working with Charlie and Rachael, although it was odd hearing them deliver our real-life dialogue. I had the opportunity to choreograph and stage the skating, and that was a good experience. Overall, when it was done, I was proud that Spectacor had made the movie. It wasn't *great*, but the filmmakers did the best that they could.

After I finished my work on the television movie, I flew east for the month of January 1990 to see how I liked living in Manhattan. Tai and I had agreed not to skate together for a while, so I gave some thought to moving to the East Coast. Between my father's death and Tai's breakdown, 1989 hadn't been a very good year for me. Perhaps a change would do me good.

John Curry, the 1976 Olympic men's champion, had turned to acting by then and was preparing to audition for the show *Jekyll and Hyde* that was in a workshop somewhere in the New York City area. During his free time John skated at Sky Rink and did a little teaching.

Like Toller Cranston, John had led the expansion of the artistic parameters of figure skating. I had always been in awe of his abilities, but he intimidated me. He was reserved and not easy to connect with. I never had gotten to know him as a friend. However, I wanted to work with somebody in New York, and who could be better than John? I took a few lessons from him. He didn't charge me a fee, which I thought was kind. When he died four years later, I felt so glad to have had that chance to work with him.

I never did move to New York, though. I remained based in Southern California. Once Tai and I got the 1980s behind us, our lives settled into a happier rhythm.

Lisa-Marie Allen

Tai and Randy always seem to have a good time. Even when things aren't going their way, they find the humor in the situation. They have such a unique relationship that they can just look at each other and giggle. Even though I am a friend of both of them, I have always felt a little bit as though I am infringing on their special bond. That connection probably has something to do with how they grew up facing adversity and managed to get through it. I love and respect each of them a great deal.

Together we opened the 1989 Atlantic City show when Tai made her comeback from problems with alcohol and depression. That was a very scary time for her. She wasn't secure. She had gone through so much. During one of the preview shows, she fell and wasn't confident enough to get up and keep going. I don't recall if she hurt herself, but she was so upset that we thought that someone had died. She ran to her dressing room, up and down three flights of stairs. I never had any concern that she would fail to make it through the run, though. She is a fighter, and so is Randy.

I didn't talk about Tai's past problems with either of them. They were never open about discussing those uncomfortable personal things. However, I think that Tai, especially now that she is a mother and has been through a failed marriage, has finally come around to realizing that the only way to heal things is to talk about them.

If you see me watching Tai and Randy perform, I always have a big smile on my face. They love what they do, and they love each other. That is very visible to me. There are so many teams, especially some of the Russian dance couples, who dislike each other. They are together, typically, for a job. It is nice to see couples who are friends and represent that when they skate.

With best friend Marina Drasnin in 1986, wearing my moon necklace.

Michael Rosenberg

There had been three to five months of no skating, when Tai and Randy were not doing anything together professionally. Nancy and I had then switched, at Randy's request, to helping him become a choreographer. He wanted to stay in skating, and he loved choreography. He thought that he would be good at it. He turned out to be great.

Six or seven months later, I got the call from Randy. "Let's put Tai and Randy back together. She thinks that she'd like to do it."

I flew to Atlantic City and stayed there with them for the first three or four nights of their engagement. I watched the show, supporting and encouraging them. It was a triumph. Tai looked great and skated beautifully. The crowds loved her more than ever—the double comeback kid.

Our 1989 comeback at Bally's in Atlantic City.

chapter five

New Perspectives, New Horizons

*T*hrough therapy, digging deep into my past, taking a break from skating, and learning to resist temptation, I conquered my demons and got ready to take a new step. At the change of the decade my life was on the brink of a radical turn for the better.

Flashback: Dorothy's show during the mid-1980s. One of the chorus skaters, Jamie Isley, had a boyfriend, a non-skater named Cary Butler. At the time he played the drums in a band. Later he became a musical engineer and producer. Cary was always around. When he came to the show to see Jamie, he enjoyed watching Dorothy, Randy, and me. He loved the backstage ice show atmosphere.

I thought of Cary as a youngster. *There's that cute young kid with the long rock 'n' roll hair.* I always had one boyfriend or another—none of them serious—so I didn't pay much attention to him.

In 1990 Cary invited me to hear his band. I went to the concert, and he was not little Cary Butler anymore. He was a beautiful young man. Very shy. He still couldn't look me in the eye. We fell in love.

After a few dates I told Cary, "Move in with me!" That was a mistake, but our life together was pretty wonderful. Very soon thereafter he asked me to marry him.

I was with Cary when *On Thin Ice*, my made-for-TV movie, was about to air. On Halloween of 1990 Randy and I appeared on Geraldo Rivera's show in a segment called "Celebrities and Drug Abuse." The next day I appeared alone on *Today* with Bryant Gumbel and Deborah Norville. When November 5, the movie's airdate, approached, I informed Cary, "We are leaving town. We are going to Santa Barbara."

Cary and I got a hotel room and watched the show together. I was a nervous wreck. I phoned my dad afterward. He was underwhelmed. He called the movie "nice." He and Mom weren't angry that I had made it, although it was true that the time since my suicide attempt had been very difficult for them. I am sure that they told themselves, "Somewhere we failed in bringing her up." It wasn't that. It wasn't that at all.

When Cary and I got home the next day, there were twenty-two messages on our answering machine from people who hadn't known how severe my problem had been. Various friends, sorry that they hadn't been there for me, left tremendously kind messages. Meg Streeter, a television producer, felt bad because she had been instrumental in the TV publicity leading up to Lake Placid. She told me, "I'm sorry if I was any part of that, making you crazy before the Games and taking up your time." All of those reactions were cathartic for me.

Randy and I were quite active during the early years I spent with Cary. At the 1991 United States Figure Skating Championships in Orlando, Florida, we were inducted into the USFSA Hall of Fame—a great honor and a nice acknowledgment as our career wound down. The induction ceremony took place between events, so there was virtually no one there to witness it. I laugh when I see the photo of us walking out onto the ice on a carpet to accept our awards. We're waving, but to whom? To Michael Rosenberg? Mr. Nicks was inducted two years later.

New Perspectives, New Horizons

That spring we played the Crystal Room at the Desert Inn Resort and Casino in Las Vegas with Linda Fratianne, Elaine Zayak, Lisa-Marie Allen, Robert Wagenhoffer, Charlene Wong, Scott Williams, Cindy Landry, Peter Oppegard, and Brian Pockar. Randy and Minnie Madden staged and directed the show, Champions on Ice. Randy and I always loved working in Las Vegas with its high energy, big crowds, and bigger budgets. The productions were topnotch. We liked the show biz feeling of the showrooms.

During the summer Randy co-directed and choreographed the Sea World show, American Spirit on Ice, while I planned my wedding.

Cary and I were married on September 29, 1991, in the Los Angeles Park Plaza Hotel, a beautiful neo-Gothic building that studios often use for film shoots. We dressed it up for a formal wedding. Cary is Jewish, so we split the ceremony half-and-half between a priest and a rabbi. I wore a lovely cream-colored gown designed by Jef Billings.

Milton Berle, who had often worked with Cary's father, Artie Butler, a well-known musical arranger and composer, was the life of the party. It was a wonderful day. All

William Daniels and Denise Nicholas on the set of On Thin Ice: The Tai Babilonia Story.

Our 1991 induction into the USFSA Hall of Fame at Nationals in Orlando, Florida.

our guests had a great time. Cary and I didn't take a honeymoon, though, because I had to go on the road with Randy not long after the wedding.

I was very pleased for Tai. I liked Cary a lot. Her previous engagement to Peter Carruthers had seemed very premature to me—both premature and immature. Then she had many boyfriends in succession, searching for distractions and changes in her life. Sometimes she moved in on them before they managed to get out "Hello. My name is …"

With Cary things were different. He came along later in the life of our partnership, when we no longer skated full-time. That was a lot easier on me.

At the same time a distressing development affected our lives. During the late 1980s the specter of AIDS had begun casting a large shadow on the skating world. Everyone knew of someone—skater, choreographer, coach—who was HIV-positive. In 1991 the tragedy became very personal for me.

Brian Pockar was my best friend. We shared a lot of common history. At the age of sixteen, Brian had come down from his home base in Calgary, Alberta, to train with Mr. Nicks during the summer. He and I had skated together as amateurs for many years.

We always got a lot of Canadians during the summer. They stayed in the beach house that Mr. Nicks rented in Malibu. Girls went nuts over Brian Pockar. Mothers went nuts. *Who is that? He's so cute. He's so talented.* From the female point of view, Brian was a nice fixture in Santa Monica.

He was definitely fun to be around: ambitious, adventurous, and inquisitive about the world. He relished experiencing new things, especially through travel, and he loved coming to Los Angeles. We often went out on the town together. He had many friends here in Southern California.

As a skater Brian was talented, versatile, and unique. He would have been so well suited to the contemporary theatrical ice shows like Gershwin on Ice and Nutcracker on Ice. He was always trying to improve as a skater, and he could do almost anything.

Brian, Tai and I once did three or four shows with Dorothy Hamill in various Alaskan cities. During practice Brian and I fooled around on the ice and decided to try some pairs moves together. I became the bottom half of a death spiral. We got into trouble for that. We were asked to leave the ice.

In the fall of 1989, during Tai's comeback, she and I worked with Brian at Bally's in Atlantic City. (We had been stepping in and out of the show, playing two weeks at a time.) Brian's stomach hurt, but he didn't know what was wrong. He told me that a local doctor hadn't been able to pinpoint the root of the pain.

One night Brian came to my hotel room between shows. He was hungry, so I said, "Why don't I order you something from room service?" He ate, but then he couldn't

A pairs move with my best friend, Brian Pockar.

skate the second show that night. Much later he admitted to me that it was during the Atlantic City run that he had been diagnosed with AIDS.

Brian didn't reveal his condition to anyone for two years. Then he came to Los Angeles for Tai's wedding. He arrived early to spend some time here, then stayed on afterward for a while. He had lost a lot of weight, and he didn't look good to me. His once-thick dark brown hair had turned completely gray.

When Tai saw Brian at the wedding, he was tan from lying in the sun. Though he was thin, she thought that he looked wonderful. He seemed to be in high spirits. He told Tai, "Tomorrow I'm going to call you at six in the morning. You're going to get up, and we'll have coffee." They did, and that was the last time that Tai ever saw him alive.

One day not long afterward Brian phoned me and said, "Randy, can I come over? I just want to walk on the beach and talk to you."

"Sure," I said. We walked along the sand, and he told me the truth.

"I don't know if you'll be surprised or not, but I have AIDS."

"Brian, I'm not surprised. I had kind of figured it out."

New Perspectives, New Horizons

By then we all could recognize the classic symptoms.

"I don't know how much time I have. My stomach hurts constantly. My vision is going. They think that maybe I have brain lesions. I wanted to come to Los Angeles to see you. I'm visiting everybody I can while I'm still able to travel."

Later Brian took a trip to Barbados. He wanted me to go with him, but I couldn't because of a schedule conflict. On April 28, 1992, seven months after Tai's wedding, he died.

It was a Tuesday evening. I was in Las Vegas, working on choreography with Minnie Madden, putting a show together. We got a call from Lisa-Marie Allen, who had heard that Brian had passed away. I happened to turn on the television news. The Rodney King riots had just erupted in Los Angeles, so I knew that there was no time to waste. I rushed home that same night.

Touch-sensitive torchière lamps lit my condominium in Marina del Rey. When I

"The Ice Stars' Hollywood Revue" with John Curry, Robin Cousins, and Liz Manley.

walked into the living room with my luggage, one of the lights was already on. It shouldn't have been.

"Wow, that's weird," I thought. Then I felt the sensation of something passing through me.

"Brian, are you here?"

The light flickered onto a brighter level.

"Okay. I thought so, Brian. I'm glad that you're here. I love you, and I miss you."

I didn't really question what I was experiencing. I felt pretty good about it, but at the same time I had a sense of awe. I walked along the hallway, sat down on my bed, and peeked around the corner.

"If you really are here, Brian, do that again."

The light flickered a second time.

I felt Brian's presence once again in the kitchen. It was like a rush of cold air going through me.

With my brother, Constancio.

Someone later told me that when people die, their spirits may pass through places that they enjoyed on earth as they make their way to heaven. I figured that Brian had just been passing by, seeing his old friends. There was a certain comfort in that thought.

The funeral service was scheduled for Saturday. Tai and I made arrangements to fly to Calgary on Thursday, but at that point the riots were in full swing, and the Los Angeles airport was closed. We telephoned various airlines, trying to get ourselves rerouted. Eventually we found a flight out of Ontario, California, an hour and one-half away. With all the ticket changing that we did, the trip turned out to be very expensive, but we simply had to go. Brian's sister had asked me to be a pallbearer. Tai and I made it to Calgary in time for the funeral, and I am so glad that we did.

It was a tough funeral, though. Watching Brian's dad suffer was particularly difficult. Toller Cranston was another of the pallbearers. Lisa-Marie Allen attended. So did Michael Rosenberg. Dorothy Hamill didn't make it.

When I came home on Saturday night after the service, there were State Troopers on top of the buildings here in Marina del Rey. The main disturbance had started to spread out from the city center toward the suburbs, and the police didn't know whether or not the local population would join in support of the downtown riots. Crowds roamed the streets. Although the local situation ended quietly, my dramatic return from Calgary was an eerie ending to an eerie week.

That was the beginning of a period of great loss in figure skating. There would be many more AIDS casualties before the epidemic abated.

Meanwhile Tai and I had been easing into a renaissance of sorts. Our career was reborn on new terms. It became less driven and more leisurely.

The November after Tai's wedding I was hired to choreograph the skating scenes for the "Fire and Ice" episode of *Beverly Hills, 90210*. While I was working, someone asked me, "Do you want to read for something?" I went upstairs and read some lines

Lisa-Marie Allen

In the early 1990s Randy did some choreography for me. He also did a lot of the staging and choreography for the Champions on Ice tours that Michael Rosenberg produced, so I had the opportunity to work with him in that context, and it was refreshing. He had an unbelievable amount of energy. He could stand on the ice for a six- or seven-hour rehearsal period and never complain about his knees or back hurting. He tried not to forget where the performer was coming from, but he was a hard worker and expected a lot. You wanted to live up to his expectations. You wanted to please him.

Randy didn't try to go for that ultimate funky thing that some people do—people who want to be so different that they are willing to stretch the limits. Randy's approach to choreography was geared to my type of skating: stylish, floaty, and airy. He listened to music with the same intent that I did, which I found comforting. Once in a while I had an unusual idea. He would think about it, and sooner or later we would come up with the choreography. That was fun.

The first year of the three-season Champions on Ice tour, 1991–92, was a classic case of survival of the fittest. We flew at horribly early hours of the morning. Some of the hotels were awful, but by the time we got to them, we were so exhausted that all we wanted to do was take a nap. Our biggest hotel problem occurred in Clearwater, Florida, where we didn't even take our bags into the rooms. We walked out and announced, "We are not staying here."

from the script. "You got the part," the casting director told me on the spot. I signed an AFTRA agreement to play the assistant coach's part. That led to Tai's hiring for a cameo role as a television commentator. The show was at the height of its popularity, and we had fun.

Then I co-directed and choreographed (with Minnie Madden) the 1991–92 World Cup Champions on Ice North American tour starring Victor Petrenko, Marina Klimova, Sergei Ponomarenko, and Lisa-Marie Allen.

Tai and I performed in Dick Clark's "Ice Stars' Hollywood Revue," filmed in Toronto during the winter of 1992. John Curry, Robin Cousins, and Liz Manley were among our fellow cast members.

I love Liz Manley to death. I have choreographed several numbers for her over the years: Tina Turner's "Proud Mary," "Itsy Bitsy Spider," and a Bryan Adams piece. She is high energy, high maintenance, and sweet. It's a different story about her love life every time you talk to her.

John Curry was in a great mood on the day when we filmed his "Ice Stars' Hollywood Revue" segment. He had taken a snapshot at the AIDS benefit that we had done together, and he told me, "Tai, I have a beautiful picture of you. I'll send you a copy." I never saw him again.

When John died two years later, I went to his memorial service in New York City. That was hard for me. It was hard for all of us in the skating world. John's mother was there, and I didn't know what to say to her. What *do* you say? I simply told her, "You have no idea what an impact your son had on me and on everyone else in skating. He is missed. His quality will never be touched."

In 1993 Randy and I celebrated our twenty-fifth anniversary as a team. We were very excited about that milestone, one that we could never have foreseen as children learning to skate. Tom Collins invited us to perform on his tour. I got myself into good shape for that one. I went to a nutritionist, followed a strict diet, and even bought new skates—anything for an edge.

The costume that I wore on that tour is one of my all-time favorites. When Randy and I met with Jef Billings to make plans, I told Jef, "I want to be naked." I was feeling pretty good about the shape that I was in, and those were the only guidelines that I gave him.

Jef came up with an amazing off-white creation. There is so much crystal on that costume! It looks like a bikini from a distance. Under spotlights no one can see all the flesh-tone mesh. Randy wore black pants and an understated black shirt with crystals on the sleeves. We plan to preserve those costumes in a Lucite display box.

I will not go out onto the ice without Jef Billings. Even when you are not in the best shape, he knows what to do. He is a genius. I adore him, as neurotic as he is—but that is an artist's nature.

Celebrating our twenty-fifth anniversary on Tom Collins's 1993 tour. (Paul Harvath, Tom Collins Enterprises)

Jef has always been a big part of Randy's and my act. We give him our music, and he plays it when he's alone in his car. I don't know how he does it, but he comes up with three or four costume sketches for us. Then we pick one. We're never disappointed.

Jef did our costumes for the 1993 Christmas season when we skated a five-week tour with a live orchestra in Nutcracker on Ice. Randy choreographed and directed that show. It closed with a run at the Aladdin Theatre for the Performing Arts. That was our first of three Nutcracker productions. We did the show again in 1995 and 1997. All three began in Mexico, then toured the United States. I played Clara. Randy played the role of the Nutcracker Prince.

In April 1994 Randy and I taped "Fox on Ice," and Randy oversaw its staging. He did another solo Sea World show that summer and worked with Karen Kresge on "Hollywood Live on Ice" for Busch Gardens in Tampa. Then he collaborated with Uschi Keszler as co-director of Elvis Stojko's Elvis Tour of Champions.

Meanwhile Cary and I wanted very much to have a baby. For two and one-half years nothing happened. Just when we were filing an adoption application, I found out that I was pregnant.

In the Gregory Peck movie *To Kill a Mockingbird*, there is a little girl named Scout. When I saw that film, I fell in love with the name. Cary and I decided, "Boy or girl, this baby is Scout."

It was an easy pregnancy for me. I was in good shape because I was doing some teaching at the rink. I kept at it until I was out to *here*. One of my students was Jack Nicholson's daughter, Lorraine. She had her father's eyes, and she reminded me of a funny little old woman. I also worked with Katia Washington, Denzel's daughter. That was fun. I gave birth just three days after I stopped teaching.

Jef Billings

I have had a long and checkered history with figure skating. I was in an elevator with Toller Cranston during Ice at Radio City in 1983. He threw an armload of costumes at me and told me that I was ruining his career.

I also designed for Peggy Fleming and Robin Cousins in Ice. Since then, I have done a lot of skating shows, including Stars on Ice. I started working with Tai and Randy during their years in Ice Capades.

It is always easier to think of a design when it is character-driven. I designed Tai and Randy's Nutcracker costumes in 1993. I had previously done a different Nutcracker for Dorothy Hamill and Gary Beacom, and there are only so many ways that you can make a costume for a soldier that looks like a nutcracker—that someone can skate in. The challenge was to make Tai's and Randy's unique.

If they are skating to just a pretty ballad, it is harder to come up with the designs. If there isn't a character involved, I will try to invent one. With "Both Sides Now," which is simply a beautiful piece of music, I said, "Let's make Tai a fairy." She had always wanted to play that character, so I arbitrarily assigned it to the costume. I didn't want to just put her in a pretty little dress.

I gave Tai sleeves that were like skirts. Randy had to learn how to work around them. He blew the fabric out of the way before he picked her up in a lift. That is the kind of thing that Tai and Randy were willing to do. I worked with other people, especially choreographers, who would have immediately said, "I can't deal with those sleeves!"

There was a pose in the *On Golden Pond* number in which Tai framed Randy with her sleeves. If the sleeves went behind Randy correctly, that was one of the prettiest photographic poses ever: a wonderful video shot at the very end of the number.

Do I ever worry that I have run out of ideas? Yes. Every time that I sit down to draw, I think that I am

Scout Gabriel Butler was born on January 25, 1995. I was thirty-five years old. Cary was twenty-nine. We were deliriously happy. After the nurses cleaned up Scout and brought him to me to hold for the first time, I whispered to him, "You are very smart, Scout." And he is. I can see it. He is a new person every single day. With his big blue eyes he seems always to be thinking.

Somehow he looks like everyone in the family. I see my dad in him. I see Cary. I see myself, especially when I look at pictures taken when I was small. This child is made up of so many nationalities and ethnic groups.

Until Scout was three years old, Cary and I didn't cut his hair. One day we told each other, "That has to be doing something to his little mind." We immediately took him for a Dutchboy haircut.

Cary, Scout, and I started our life together in a condo in Santa Monica. Soon an irresistible opportunity came along. When I first turned professional, I bought my parents a corner house in Sherman Oaks. One day a neighbor around the corner and two houses down the street told my father, "I'm putting my house up for sale in a few days."

Dad said, "Tai and Cary are looking," and that was that. We bought the house and moved in.

I loved living close to my mother, and I still do. We watch over each other. Scout adores visiting Grandma. At Grandma's house he can do *anything*. Grandma doesn't say no the way Mommy does.

My marriage to Cary lasted only four years. He really wanted to make our marriage work, but I couldn't give enough of myself. My life had been so different from his. I

never going to have another new idea. Then one emerges. Lots of times the ideas come to me in my car when I am driving and listening to music. I am a captive audience then, and I'm not distracted. Lightning doesn't come down from the sky and strike me with insight. I have various people who call me when they have new fabrics and this and that. Then I play with ideas, and the costumes evolve.

There is a woman who used to work at Courtney's who semi-retired several years ago. She basically now builds everything that I design. She sews all of the Stars on Ice costumes and all my private work. She can do anything.

Of course skating involves special demands. I have never had problems with how my costumes are constructed, so I don't tend to ask about the minute details. Some seams are overlocked with a stretch-stitch machine. Some seams are double-stitched. If things are fit properly, they don't absorb much strain.

Kids always say that their pants have to stretch. Well, they skate in jeans all the time. That is because the crotch in a pair of jeans is high. In a regular pair of dress pants with a low crotch, you couldn't raise your legs. The secret of clothes for skating is in the cut and the fabric.

Some professional skaters haven't quite made the full transition from amateurism. In many cases that is because they don't want to spend the money to collaborate with a professional costume designer in presenting a polished overall package. They don't think that it is important to do so because they have no idea what a difference a professional designer can make in presentation. Besides, they have a feeling that when a professional does a costume, it costs so much more. That isn't necessarily true. I have heard through the grapevine that some skaters have spent fifteen hundred dollars for costumes that look like twelve dollars. If you spend a thousand, you should look like a million.

With Jef Billings.

had been on my own so much. I had lived so much more intensely.

I moved back home with my parents around the corner, and Cary stayed in our house until he was ready to buy a home of his own nearby. Then I went back to living on my own.

Cary and I made an agreement to keep our divorce as simple and pleasant for Scout as we could, and the arrangement works. Scout gets love from all around. He splits the week between my house and his father's, so he has two loving homes, two great bedrooms (plus one at Grandma's), and two sets of toys.

Cary remarried a few years ago. He and his wife have a two-year-old son, and they just added a baby girl to their family. Scout is going through all those changes: being the big brother and finding his place in the mix. He's doing great. He's seven now, and he's a wonderful reader. He plays the guitar. He's taking tae kwon do lessons. Incredible!

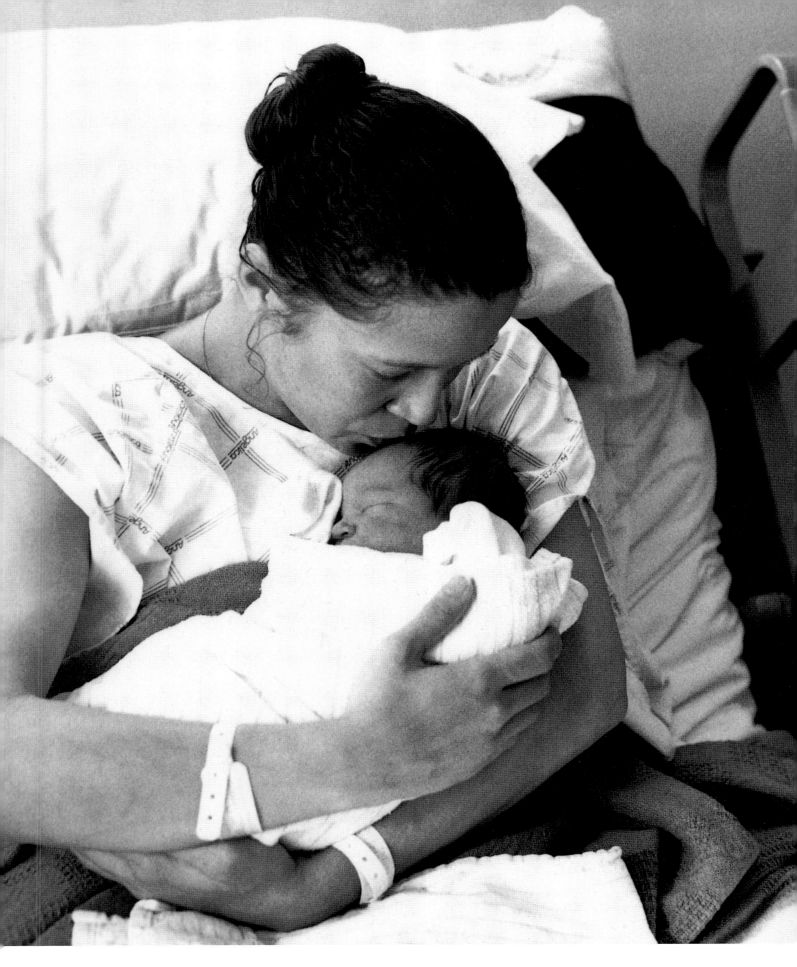

Scout Gabriel Butler on January 25, 1995.

Like many children, Scout is extremely fond of dressing up in character, but he is one of the few kids in the world who has his Halloween costumes designed by Jef Billings. He doesn't know what a lucky boy he is.

Scout and I are best friends. One day I told him, "Scout, you are going to end up taking care of Mommy. You know that, don't you? When I'm old and senile, I'll be right there with you."

He is strong and fiercely independent. I believe that trait comes from me. I tell him everything. I even talk to him about the divorce. "This is how it is. Mommy and Daddy are just better off separate, so you have two separate houses. That's pretty special. Not every child has that."

A typical road scene: sleeping on the bus.

If Cary and I are fighting, I tell Scout what we are fighting about. Kids get it. They know when something is wrong, so why hide it? Scout is the light at the end of the tunnel for me. He motivates me in everything that I do. Even my skating changed for the better because of him.

While Scout was a baby and a toddler, Randy and I didn't work much together. That was just as well, because I was able to spend a lot of time with my parents. Throughout 1995, the year of my divorce, I began to notice that something was wrong with my dad. All of a sudden he got weak. He was losing his balance a lot of the time. He was dropping weight, gaining it back, and then dropping it again. It seemed very strange because he had always been so strong and tough. Nothing could knock him down. We all knew that there was a problem, but we didn't know what it was.

I noticed that my dad started doing things that he had never done before. He drove to San Diego with my mom and my brother. He insisted on dropping everything and going to Mexico at Christmas when Randy and I performed in Nutcracker on Ice. It was great to have him there. He became a fixture on that tour. He did many things that were out of character for him. It was almost as though he knew that his time was limited, but we didn't talk about that. He was having fun—finally.

In August of 1996, my dad went into the hospital with heart problems. It was the same Hollywood hospital, Kaiser Permanente on Sunset Boulevard, where I had been born almost thirty-seven years earlier.

One morning about a week later, Cary happened to be at my mom's house checking on Scout when the telephone rang. Mom and I were in the living room, so Cary answered the phone. I don't know what the nurse told him, but the message that he relayed to us was "Get right over to the hospital." My dad had been walking from the bathroom to the bed when he collapsed from a pulmonary embolism, a blood clot in the lungs. When we arrived, he had already died.

They put him on his bed, and I curled up next to him. He was still warm. I had a conversation with him. Randy and I had some pro competitions coming up in the fall, and I asked my dad, "Should I still go?" Something told me that I ought to do the events because that would make him happy. They were all going to be televised, and my dad had always loved to see Randy and me on TV.

Returning to competition was a big thing because people hadn't seen us in a while. We did Legends, another Mike Burg competition, and Dick Button's U.S. Pro in Albany, New York, knowing that we weren't going to win. But it got Randy and me back on television, and we were able to let people know that we were still around.

In some weird way, skating those competitions was the perfect outlet for my grief. That was probably some of the most emotional work that Randy and I have done together. Peggy Fleming was the commentator for the first of the three events. The day before we performed, I called Peggy and told her, "I'd like to dedicate the number that we're doing tomorrow night to my father." We skated to the Kenny Loggins song "Love," and it was really special. I put everything I had into that performance.

At about the same time, Randy worked on a new Elvis tour and choreographed Las

Vegas on Ice. Then he and I performed again on Tom Collins's winter tour during January and February of 1997. We have been lucky in our careers. Many great people like Tom Collins have believed in us and have repeatedly given us opportunities over the years.

When our first coach, Mabel Fairbanks, was elected to membership in the USFSA Hall of Fame, Randy and I were so happy for her. I bought her an outfit to wear to her induction at the 1997 Nationals in Nashville, Tennessee. Mabel always loved to sparkle, so I thought that a big, sparkly jacket would be perfect for her. The one that I chose had lots of gold and glittery jewel tones. The jacket went over a black dress, so I said, "Mabel, just wear black pumps."

"No," she replied. "I want to sparkle all over." She wore a pair of multicolored jeweled pumps that were fancier than Dorothy's ruby slippers.

I had the privilege of escorting her out onto the ice. She was a hit that night, especially when the announcer recounted the story of her younger days as the woman who revolutionized figure skating for minorities. When people heard about her struggles and triumphs, they went nuts and gave her a standing ovation. They swarmed her for autographs. That was a highlight of Mabel's life—and of mine, too.

That summer Randy and I played three Los Angeles dates on the Tom Collins tour and did some publicity work. *Finally* we got to appear on *The Tonight Show*. We had wanted to do that ever since 1980. Eventually dreams do come true. Jay Leno impressed us. He was clever, and he worked hard. We taped our skit at the Pickwick Arena in Burbank. Jay had us cut a pizza with our skate blades.

During the years when I was especially preoccupied with Scout, Randy kept very busy as a private choreographer and producer. For several seasons he also worked for Tom Collins. He helped Tommy put together the opening and the finale of his annual Tour of World and Olympic Champions (later renamed Champions on Ice), set the running order of the show, got the skaters on and off the ice, and kept everyone calm.

He became a babysitter at times, too, because there were so many different personalities within the sometimes-volatile international cast, from the highest-strung artistic personalities, *way* up in the air, all the way down to the mellow end of the spectrum. Randy rode the buses with the cast and sometimes ended up as the unofficial peacekeeper. *There are a lot of shows left, guys. Just hold on.* The skaters admired him. He is very good with people.

During the summer of 1997 I had my work cut out for me with Oksana Baiul. She was having problems with alcohol abuse and emotional instability. I was in charge of "general maintenance" throughout the tour. As director of staging I flew in and out to make sure that things were running smoothly: music, lighting, as well as personal concerns.

Sarah Kawahara had choreographed Oksana's numbers, and she asked me to watch over Oksana whenever possible during the course of the tour. That entailed overseeing her warm-ups and making sure that she practiced certain moves and maintained a

Sparkling all over.

Mabel's 1997 induction into the USFSA Hall of Fame.

In the summer of 1997 we finally got to do The Tonight Show with Jay Leno. (Matthew J. Lee, Long Beach Press Telegram)

high performance level. Through our student/teacher relationship, Oksana and I grew close to one another as friends.

One evening Oksana was doing her usual pre-show routine: pacing back and forth listening to the Walkman on her head. A middle-aged woman approached me and told me that she adored Miss Baiul. Could I arrange for her to obtain an autograph and take a photo?

I went to get Oksana. After great resistance on her part and much persuasion on mine, I brought Oksana to meet her fan. The woman was waiting at the end of a long hallway, pen and paper in hand. Oksana signed her name, then pulled away abruptly.

"She wants your picture, too," I explained. Oksana backed up farther and tried to get away.

"Just stand still for two seconds while this woman snaps a picture."

Oksana moved toward the woman, then pulled back. Again she moved forward, then retreated. All the while the poor woman was constantly refocusing her camera. Finally Oksana went nearly face to face, stared for a moment, stuck out her tongue, and gave the woman a rude raspberry. Then she ran back down the hall, laughing hysterically. That was not a happy time for Oksana.

It was during that same summer that Tai and I first became involved with Camp Laurel, a year-round program for children living with HIV and AIDS. The camp, a brainchild of Margot Andrew, got off the ground in 1993 as a small summer program, free of charge to qualified children between the ages of six and sixteen. Since then Camp Laurel has come to encompass three additional seasonal camping experiences plus monthly outings in the Los Angeles area.

Tai's and my involvement began with a skating party. Then the foundation's honorary board of directors accepted us as members. Many of the participants in the Camp Laurel program are minority children who were born with HIV infections, most likely because their parents were drug abusers. Some have lost their parents. Others are second-generation victims of transfusions with infected blood. Tai and I get a lot of satisfaction and pleasure from working with the charity. It's a way to honor the memories of friends like Brian Pockar, John Curry, and Robert Wagenhoffer.

Randy and I launched our thirtieth anniversary year, the swan song of our touring career, on a high note. During the 1997–98 holiday season we appeared at the Aladdin Theatre in Las Vegas in Nutcracker on Ice—my favorite piece of work to date. I loved Clara, the little girl in the story. I struggled in playing her again, doubting that I could pull it off at the age of thirty-eight. I became drained trying to capture her, but it was the most rewarding work that I have ever done. I am so glad that Randy and I got to launch our special year that way.

We had a proscenium stage, which I love more than anything. I like being able to see and feel the people in the audience. That type of show is always more creative for me than when we skate around on Olympic-size ice. Yes, the small size limits us, but we can tell our stories better when we are closer to the audience.

Another dream came true that same December when Randy and I performed in Gershwin on Ice with Peggy Fleming and Rudy Galindo. Peggy has so much class. Working with her was a dream. The real excitement of it didn't hit me until after we had finished. We worked for a week—got on the ice, got off—and that was it. When the run was over, I stopped and thought, "You just worked with your idol. Hello!"

Rudy is amazing, too. I watched him on television when he won the 1996 Nationals in San Jose, and I was so proud of him. He overcame a lot in his life.

Rudy Galindo is a good friend of mine. Tai and I watched him train with Kristi Yamaguchi. They were a great pairs team. I thought that they would be the next Tai and Randy.

Then Kristi decided that she would be better off focusing on singles. Obviously that was a good career move for her. She became the world and Olympic champion. But she didn't maintain contact with Rudy at a time when he was fighting for his career. He had to ride his bicycle to the rink because he didn't have a car. He had to accept free lessons from his sister, Laura. Kristi knew about Rudy's problems, and I was disappointed that she didn't step forward to help him out. Every time I watch the tape of him winning Nationals, I get chills all over again.

Backstage with Tom Bradley. Tom was good to us during his years as mayor of Los Angeles.

Gershwin on Ice in December 1997 with Peggy Fleming and Rudy Galindo.

Celebrating our thirtieth year together on the 1998 Tom Collins tour.

I did some choreography for Rudy after he turned professional. The first piece was a classical piano version of "Ice Castles" that emphasized his long lines and stretch. He used that number a lot on the Tom Collins tour and at competitions. Then I did "Morning Has Broken," which didn't turn out as well. Neither one of us liked it. I believe that he performed it only once. Then I choreographed an *a cappella* version of "The Rose" by the Fleet Street Singers, a Bay Area group.

Rudy sometimes works with a very good dance choreographer. He moves well, and he can do anything that a choreographer asks of him. He is artistic and highly emotional. However, he also has a lot of preconceived ideas of what he ought to do, and I don't always agree with his choices.

Because many opportunities came our way in 1998, Tai held out the hope that we could mark our thirtieth anniversary season with a television special and a book deal. Those things didn't happen. As for myself, I just felt lucky that we were still skating together after all those years. I didn't give a damn who else knew. It was a personal triumph for me that we had made it. I had plenty of videos and scrapbooks. Those thirty years formed a chapter of my life that I was very proud of.

The reality was that the networks weren't going to buy a Tai and Randy thirtieth anniversary show when Michelle Kwan and Tara Lipinski had just won medals at the 1998 Olympics. The show would have been great to do, but it wasn't going to happen. Tai had a hard time understanding that and accepting it, so she left Michael Rosenberg and found new representation. I stayed on with Michael.

Tai does get bored quickly. She believes that she outgrows things and people—like her marriage and her boyfriends. She told me, "I think that we've outgrown Michael." That was fine. She was happy with her new agent. He quickly came up with several job offers for her.

The culmination of our thirtieth-anniversary year was one last Tom Collins tour. Tommy has always been one of our angels. Randy and I were on his very first tour more than twenty years ago, and we did many of those tours over the years. Tommy invited us again because he knew that 1998 was going to be special for us. With all the other skating talent that he had lined up, he didn't really need us, but he cared about us, and he knew that we would have fun.

Linda Fratianne

Tai, Randy, and I did Nutcracker on Ice together in Atlantic City. We had a set time to rehearse for forty-five minutes to an hour—just the three of us before the show. Tai and Randy were always together, always on time, always rested and professional. It is not easy doing ten or twelve shows a week. There is an incredible chemistry between them, on and off the ice.

When my daughter, Alexandra, was six months old and just starting to pull herself up, Tai, Randy, and I were working at the Desert Inn in Las Vegas. Tai was in my dressing room one day with a Polaroid camera, and she got the first picture of Ali standing up. Now that Tai has a baby, it is so much fun. We can relate to each other, mother to mother. Ali's birthday is the same as Tai's.

I am close to Randy in a different way. Girls tend to talk about deeper things. Randy is very professional and a wonderful, dear friend. I can't say enough good things about him. We have all had a ball together.

(Michon Halio)

Nutcracker on Ice …

(Michon Halio)

Christmas 1997

Backstage at Nutcracker on Ice with Jack Nicholson and his children.

Randy and I never imagined that we would still be together thirty years after that first skate around the rink in Culver City when we didn't want to hold hands. If we had thought about the future at all, I suppose that we would have expected to continue for several years past the Olympics, then go our separate ways. Instead we formed a lasting bond that deepened over time.

Of all our Collins tours, I enjoyed the 1998 winter tour the most. We wore red and skated to "Going to the Chapel." The experience got better and better as the cities flew by. I didn't let the pressure bother me. Performing had become secondary in my life in the context of motherhood. I could just relax and have fun.

The downside was that it was hard being away from Scout. Cary brought him to visit me on tour. It was great that Cary and I got along well enough that he could do that kind of thing for me. We were pretty lucky. That doesn't always happen in a divorce.

Our last city on the tour was West Palm Beach. You get a certain feeling when you realize that that's it—the very last one. I knew in my heart that Randy and I couldn't keep going forever. When is it *enough*? We had done everything that we wanted to do in our careers. It was time to move on to the next chapter.

When I got home, Scout was angry with me. His reaction was not pleasant. *I love you. I hate you. I love you. I hate you*. It took time for us to forge a strong bond again. I was very protective of Scout. He came first.

Randy and I didn't swear off performing. We just stopped touring. We might still accept a television special if we knew about it well in advance. At our ages it takes us a while to get back into shape and pull everything together.

After Tai and I left the tour as performers, I continued to fly in from time to time in my role as performance director. In April 1998, while checking on the show in Washington, D.C., I went to dinner at the home of a friend named Cathy. Her husband, Tom, is a U.S. marshal. During the height of the Clinton investigation, Tom was assigned to protect special prosecutor Kenneth Star. You could glimpse him on television when Star made his morning trip to the car with his cup of coffee.

Tom and Cathy planned to see the show the next day, so I told them, "Here's what we should do."

Tommy Collins was having trouble getting work visas for the Russian skaters—nearly half the cast. They were skating with visitors' visas. I explained the situation to Tom. Then we discussed Rudy Galindo's conviction for driving under the influence of alcohol several years earlier. Tom wrote down everything that I told him.

He and a friend, another marshal, appeared at the arena the following afternoon during practice. They asked for me, and the unwitting arena security guards called me on their walkie-talkies. When I met Tom and his friend at the Security command post, they flashed their badges and informed me with straight faces, "We need to see whoever is in charge here." Guns and holsters were visible beneath their suit coats.

A security guard contacted the backstage area. Our stage manager, Paul Hendrickson, came out and asked, "Is there a problem?"

"Who's in charge here?"

"That would be Tom Collins."

When Tommy and his son, Michael, appeared with Lou, our security man, the two marshals flashed their badges again.

"We have a couple of problems here. We need to see you privately."

The group disappeared into a room and shut the door. They wouldn't let me in. That annoyed me, but I listened at the door. Meanwhile rumors flew. *Somebody is in with the bosses. What's going on?*

Inside the closed room Tom informed Tommy, "We understand that you have some Russian skaters working without visas. The government can shut your show down immediately."

Since that was perfectly true, it sounded authentic. Tommy and Michael were devastated. How had the immigration department found out? They began sweating and fumbling.

"Well, we have the paperwork back at the hotel. We're staying in Baltimore, but we can have it sent down here."

Then the marshals brought up the issue of interstate transportation of minors—Tara Lipinski and Michelle Kwan.

"No, no. Their parents are here. They're with the girls all the time."

Finally the marshals made point number three.

"We need to see Mr. Galindo."

Tom had Rudy brought into the room.

"Mr. Galindo, is your sister, Laura, here?"

"No, she's at home."

"Well, we need to speak with her. We understand that you have violated the terms of your probation."

Rudy was confused.

"I don't have probation anymore. I've finished my community service."

At that point I walked in laughing. *What is he laughing about? This is serious!* Then the marshals announced, "You know what? You've all just been had by Randy Gardner."

Tommy and Michael were so mad—mad but relieved. They always pulled tricks like that themselves. They were such jokesters. It was fun to turn the tables on them for a change.

Tommy told me, "Gardner, your day will come."

In a sense it did—later in 1998. I was disappointed in how my relationship with the Collinses ended. It was the oddest thing. It caught me totally off-guard. I heard through the rumor mill that Tommy was going to hire a different choreographer. I decided, "I'll check out the rumor. I'm going to see him tonight."

Tommy was very cavalier about the situation.

"Yeah, yeah, yeah, I'm going to try someone else."

"Was there a problem?"

"No, there was nothing wrong with your work. I'm just going to explore with other people."

That was fine. What bothered me was that I didn't learn the truth until July when the show played Los Angeles, yet Tommy had talked to the new choreographer, Sarah Kawahara, back in May during the New York date. He had known about the change for two months and probably had been scared to tell me about it. Instead he avoided the issue. I had been on the road with him, off and on, for more than twenty years. I was just disappointed that he hadn't come to tell me himself.

I had always done what he wanted me to do. Still, when he decided to go with someone else, that was fine. I am in a transient career. Producers don't always keep choreographers year after year. I can understand that. That is why we do one-year or two-year deals.

I suspect that Tommy regrets now that I found out through the rumor mill. He told me, "Randy, I will have you back."

Okay. But do I want to come back?

The situation didn't affect our friendship, but you live and learn. Certain people aren't always up-front and honest. Once you realize that, you can deal with them on those terms. The fact remains that Tom Collins is a very generous man. He has employed almost every skating champion on the planet. His generosity has served him well. We all will skate for Tommy at the drop of a hat.

I see my future in choreography and production. I enjoy overseeing projects. I surround myself with talented people—the set designer, the costumer—and tell them, "Here is what I want to do with the number. There will be this many people. They're going to move a lot. They're going to be dancing 1940s (or whatever the style may be)." Then I let those creative people go off by themselves. I never say, "I want blue pants with a belt." That way the creative people can surprise me.

Originally my choreographic work was intricate. I got that tendency from my mentor, Sarah Kawahara, and sometimes I went overboard. Now that I have incorporated some of my own approaches into my work, I am more laid back than I was. I know more about myself, and I get things done faster.

One of my most entertaining projects was a nationwide commercial spot for the National Hockey League, "NHL on Fox." I basically cast a chorus line of hockey skaters. About one hundred high school, junior, and pro hockey players from the Los Angeles area showed up for the audition. I chose the twenty who were the quickest and most agile and who had the best sense of rhythm. They showed up for the shoot in full gear. I choreographed precision moves for them to the sounds of their blades and the tapping of their sticks. Afterward we overdubbed music from *West Side Story*.

I have worked with many of the world's top figure skaters on an individual basis. Tonia Kwiatkowski was great to work with when I choreographed Mannheim Steamroller's "The Christmas Angel" for NBC. She was fresh and new to professional skating, and she didn't have preconceived ideas. She was so enthusiastic about everything that we did.

It was also an honor to work with Dorothy Hamill on that show after being her friend for so many years. I hadn't dealt with her professionally since the Festival on Ice shows in the late 1980s. I also enjoyed working with her personal choreographer, Tim Murphy, whom I knew as a skater. Dorothy and Tim came in with her solo work already set. Then Tim collaborated with me in putting Dorothy into the production numbers.

I like Tim's work as a choreographer. He is the one who really developed Dorothy's look and line during the 1990s. She is one of the originals. There is nobody like her with respect to flow, strength, bearing, and the way she takes the ice. All she has to do is skate by with an edge, and people applaud. She has always had that special quality, but Tim showcased it in her work. I get a chill when I watch her. Other women nowadays don't have that quality—except Michelle Kwan.

There is one job I was offered that I did not accept. Michael Rosenberg briefly represented Tonya Harding. "Why?" is what I wanted to know when he told me. Tonya was skating again, and Michael had booked a competition for her, the 1999 Pro Skating Championships in Huntington, West Virginia. Michael was hoping to also produce a full-scale extravaganza with Tonya as the headliner, possibly in Las Vegas or Atlantic City.

But the Tonya/Nancy hoopla was over. Nobody really cared anymore. Michael wanted me to choreograph Tonya's show. I said no.

"We've got to give Tonya a second chance."

"We do?"

"Mike Tyson got a second chance."

"Mike Tyson served time."

"Tonya wasn't convicted."

"O.J. Simpson wasn't convicted either, but I'm not working with him."

Many people maintain that Tonya lied and was more involved in the attack on Nancy Kerrigan than she led us all to believe.

Nancy is an attractive skater. Nancy is great. But although she was somewhat famous before the 1994 incident in Detroit, she really shot to fame because of it. Tonya/Nancy boosted the skating business 200 percent. Now, the greater part of a decade later, we are back to where we started. The positive effect has all worn off. Overexposure killed the boom. People aren't buying. People don't care. Business is poor. Tonya/Nancy wasn't necessarily bad for skating, but it gave us, as a sport, an exaggerated collective sense of self. Now we are back to reality.

Tai and I have had some production ideas of our own. We enjoy working together as a team. We both believe that there is room today for more artistic skating—more creative and production-oriented than the pro-ams and exhibitions that the networks are buying.

Randy and I want to always work together. It doesn't have to be as skating partners. After this long we can't just drop each other. I have my own creative ideas, although I don't know as much about business as Randy does.

Choreography isn't in me, however. Either you have the knack or you don't. When I was working with children, I knew that I didn't have what it took to create patterns. If someone else choreographs a number, I am good at cleaning it up, adding the finishing touches. That was what I did when I taught. *Tai, here's a number. Make it shiny.* I loved that.

Randy has always been an upbeat, stable person. I don't know how he manages. He just doesn't let problems get to him—or if they do get to him, he doesn't let me see that. He keeps his private life very private. Nothing needs to be said. He wants it that way, and I respect his wishes.

But if I want to cry, I cry. If I feel something, I go with the emotion. I kept things bottled up for so many years, and that didn't work for me. Better for me to let it out right away than to hold it in just to keep the peace. Maybe that is how Randy is different from me, or maybe he vents in a different manner.

Tai is more complicated than I am. I believe that women in general are more complicated. I'm going to get clobbered for saying so, but most men I know are a little more even-keeled than the majority of women.

I have gotten better at sharing my feelings, though. I used to be very closed. Then I developed an ulcer about ten years ago when I was involved intensively in choreography.

The condition was diagnosed during a show that I was working on, Michael Rosenberg's World Cup Figure Skating Champions. Then I realized that I had to express my feelings more. I was perfectly happy, but I had internalized my job stress. After years of that, an ulcer was probably inevitable.

Maybe that is where the balance is with us. If I were like Randy, or if he were like me, we might not have succeeded. There is some special chemistry that has worked.

I am not impractical, but I think that I am more of a free spirit than Randy is. *It doesn't have to get done today. I can do it tomorrow.* I am much more on top of things now. The fact that I am currently wearing a watch took a lot of effort on Randy's part. I didn't care what time it was. *I'll get there. I'll find a clock in a bank or something. I'll ask the gas station man.* I always did get where I was going—half an hour late. I like the freedom to be a little bit late. Virgos on the whole are quite well organized, but in some areas I don't want to be. I couldn't hold a nine-to-five job. I would be fired immediately.

Randy told me, "If you are going to produce with me, you can't be the way you used to be. You have to answer the phone. You have to call people back. You have to wear a watch. You have to get a fax machine, and eventually you will have to get a computer. That's how we do things here. That's what it is to be a producer."

A computer? I thought that the fax machine was bad enough. But Randy was right. You have to have some sort of organization. That is a big thing for me these days. When you have a child to care for, organization definitely helps. It takes me a while to *get* something, but once I get it, I never forget it. Now I even have an e-mail address.

Tai doesn't have a lot of executive stamina. She is not as tough as nails. She can't understand why certain decisions must be made. I have occasionally been disappointed in her when she has made decisions based upon her emotions rather than upon her intellect. I am a careful planner. I think things through and react to the big picture. Tai acts on the emotions of the moment. Sometimes that leads to mistakes, but she learns from them.

Tai has gotten much stronger over the years. Marriage and having a child developed her as a woman and as a person. She is self-assured and has her priorities in order. True, she operates on intuition, but she has the best insights. Sometimes when Tai tells me about an idea, my initial reaction is "What?" But most of the time she is right.

For example, one night a number of years ago, when Tai couldn't sleep, she called on her late father, Connie, for inspiration.

"Dad, what should I do? I have to do something with my life. You've got to help me out."

She heard a voice in her mind telling her to call the owner of a line of clothing that she liked to wear. She picked up the phone the next day, called the guy, met with him, and got her deal. Now she is putting her name on a line of skatewear.

Champions on Ice.

Designing a clothing line is something that I had wanted to do for six or seven years. While watching practice sessions, I had noticed that there was a need for good skating clothes for fifteen-year-olds up to women my age and older. There is really nothing in the skating catalogues that is flattering or comfortable for older women who have hips and boobs and who like to keep certain parts of their bodies covered.

The women in the coffee club were wearing sweats or finding ballet skirts in dance-wear stores, but there was nothing flowing and beautiful that made them feel great while they skated. I thought, "There's a market here, and I want to tap into it."

I reached the point of really wanting to make the dream happen. In the middle of the night, something told me to call a downtown company called Mica. I had worn their clothes for years: ladies' fine apparel, beautiful evening gowns and street dresses. I made the call myself and pitched my idea to the owner, Denny Rabineau. He thought that it was interesting. He had never been involved in skating himself, but he had been a fan of Randy's and mine for a long time.

Denny and I put together a sample line. The clothes have a simple, classical ballet look. There are wonderful chiffon skirts in pastel colors and deep jewel tones—burgundies, blues, and greens—really luscious. Simple little wrap sweaters come in coordinating colors. Those are the types of clothes I rehearse in. They're very comfortable, and you always look good.

I admire Tai's spontaneity, her ability to act on an impulse, like the impulse that led her to make that phone call to Mica. I have worked to acquire some of that spontaneity myself.

Christopher Knight

During the twenty years that intervened between Tai's and my first meeting and our recent reacquaintance, I had my ups and downs—possibly more downs than ups. In 1980 I had already been making decisions for myself for a number of years, but I still had a lot of growth and experiences to go through. During that passage Tai's growth paralleled mine. Hers was just a little more public.

What is amazing is that, with all the hard lessons that she has had to learn, there is still that virginal sparkle that I first saw in her. There is a part of her that hasn't been touched by all that's she's been through. She has led a full life. She has had a lot of experiences, not all of them fulfilling, but she's not worn by them. And she had to put everything together for herself. She did a wonderful job.

In those twenty years, I lost touch with Tai. I got married—twice. A couple of times between marriages,

I spoke with Tai and caught up with her, but then she was married herself, or about to get married. Luckily she found a special person, and they subsequently made a family. That's probably when the real woman was able to find herself.

A number of years ago I received a letter from Tai. She was reaching out, in good counseling fashion. It wasn't an entirely happy note. It revealed her frustration. *Why can't we be friends? Why can't we communicate?* I was married at the time, and I was afraid that my wife wouldn't understand. Our bond wasn't secure enough for me to make that kind of connection with someone else. I needed to maintain a distance. But I kept the letter, although it was rather confusing to me—as was her movie of the week.

During the summer of 1980 I bought Tai a teeny little ring. As I found out recently, she has it still. Seeing that ring again was tantamount to going back to

Tai and I balance each other out by bringing different qualities to our relationship. During the past five years we have been realistic about ourselves as people and as skaters, and we haven't been afraid to voice our feelings to each other. Like all good relationships, ours requires honesty, openness, integrity, and compromise.

When we were children, Tai and I took each other for granted. Now we do lots of things together that we didn't do when we were younger. Sometimes we go to shows or events together. Tai tells me things and listens to what I have to say. She likes to share the latest with me. I am her best friend. That friendship developed over the years because of everything that we went through as a unit. In becoming adults, we realized how important we were to one another.

Now more than ever I call Randy just to talk, run things past him, and ask his advice. We have been through so much together. I always talk to him about my boyfriends and this and that. He is the same way with me.

When we stopped performing on the ice regularly, our relationship became more relaxed. We got to know each other as people. Randy saw different sides of me, and I saw different sides of him, which was nice. We no longer had the pressure of skating. We were just two people trying to make a living, trying to help each other get through life happily and successfully.

elementary school and seeing the little desk that I once sat in. The ring didn't seem so little at the time! It's just a chip of a diamond inside a heart. I bought it for Tai before she left for Ice Capades, in the hope that maybe she'd remember me when she was off on her journey. Apparently she did.

There is a commonality between Tai and me. We have seen highs, seen lows, persevered, and made ourselves into better people in the process. That commonality helps us to connect. Tai can appreciate what I've been through, and I can certainly appreciate what she's been through.

About twelve years ago I left the pursuit of acting as a career. Now I'm in the high tech industry. I'm one of the founders of a start-up company in San Jose. It is a totally different approach to life but one that is self-driven. Being an actor is so much an *effect*. You're part of somebody else's puzzle.

My dad was an actor. I wasn't so much smitten by that dream. Dreams can be nightmares. What I wanted was a comfortable home, the white picket fence thing. I didn't need recognition. In fact, I was always uncomfortable with it—as I think Tai is. She doesn't seem to have a burning need to be recognized. She, like me, wants to have a comfortable life. With all the attention that she's had, she hasn't really bought into its importance.

Tai almost looks younger than when I first met her. She certainly looks happier. She's involved in life and still growing. I'm very happy to see, not just that she has weathered the storm as well as she has, but that it has made her an incredibly beautiful person.

angdon)

epilogue

Return to Lake Placid

After 1980 Randy and I were asked back to Lake Placid two or three times to perform exhibitions. We always shied away from them. Conveniently other things came up. We really weren't ready. There still was something very scary for both of us about returning to the scene of our trauma. We didn't discuss what scared us. We just never did it. We always found some excuse not to go back.

In late 1999 Tom Collins called to invite us to judge the Winter Goodwill Games in February 2000 in Lake Placid: twenty years, almost to the day, since our Olympics. We talked to each other and agreed, "So much time has passed. We're grown-ups. We don't have to skate. We're just going to judge a competition."

I wasn't at all nervous before we left for Lake Placid. *It's going to be fine. Let's just go and do it.* I wasn't approaching the trip as the Big Return to Lake Placid. But when I got there, it *was* the Big Return to Lake Placid.

We flew out of Los Angeles and made a stop somewhere in between to connect to another flight. I was sitting in the boarding lounge waiting to get on our plane when I glanced over at the other passengers and saw what I thought at first was a cute little girl dressed all in denim. She might have been twelve years old. Then I recognized her. *Kitty?*

It was Kitty Carruthers. She was on her way to judge the Goodwill Games, too, so the three of us flew to Albany together. A car took us up to the remote Lake Placid Village in the Adirondack Mountains of northern New York State. The trip seemed to take forever. It was cold and dark. Then we arrived in the center of the hamlet. *Oh, my gosh, this is it.* It seemed tiny compared to what I remembered. The streets and the shops were all so close together and small. In 1980 the place had seemed big and crowded. Now it was completely different.

We drove right by the Olympic Centre. I thought nervously, "Oh, there it is" and just sort of glanced at it as we passed. Then we were at our hotel, the Golden Arrow, across the street from the arena, with the frozen, snow-covered Mirror Lake at its back.

The next day we went to watch the practices, something that the organizers had advised the judges to do. The gathering of the judging panel became a major reunion. Robin Cousins, Gordy McKellen, Irina Rodnina, JoJo Starbuck, Charlie Tickner, and of course Kitty were all there. We sat in the stands, greeting each other, laughing while the skaters practiced. *I can't believe that they're doing this. How did we do it?* I expected to feel emotional and sad, but the experience was just the opposite, probably because I was constantly laughing with Robin, Gordy, and Charlie. My stomach muscles actually ached by the end of the evening.

Dorothy Hamill was out there on the ice. She was probably the one skater closest to us in age, from our era. It was really nice to see her. She looked great and skated beautifully.

Epilogue

I felt like a little kid once again, especially with Gordy there. I turned into the fourteen-year-old girl I used to be, laughing just as hard at some of the silliest things. For me, that made the bogeyman leave the arena. As we sat watching the practices, Randy told me, "I'm going to take a walk." *Okay, he's taking a walk.* I think that he went and relived everything. I let him go alone. That lap around the Olympic Centre was something that he had to do.

When I first entered the building through those big glass doors to the left of the practice rink and in front of the main arena, all the memories came back like a chill.

Later I took a little stroll by myself. I saw the corner of the hallway where we sat between the warm-up and our turn to compete. Then I tried to find the locker rooms where we got dressed and the one where I received the shot of Xylocaine, but I couldn't pinpoint them. I went into *all* of the locker rooms. A lot of them resembled each other, and I couldn't differentiate among them.

I saw the exit where we walked off the ice for the last time. The practice rink brought back memories, too: skating in that facility with the injury, wondering what was going to happen. I just stood there and let all the feelings come back. I'm glad that I did it. It was cathartic. It got me over a hump, and it closed the chapter on that part of my life.

I hit all the same places, too, because you just do in the normal course of walking through the Olympic Centre. *Okay, here's the dressing room.* The 1980 rink itself, like the whole village, was smaller than I thought it would be. I remembered the seats going up much higher. When I got inside, I realized, "No, everything is so low. There aren't that many rows of seats." I tried to remember the seat where my mom sat, and I vaguely recalled her section across from the judges.

The two things that stood out the most for me were the door to the dressing room and the entrance onto the ice. But seeing those places again wasn't really emotional for me. I simply had brief flashbacks. I kept telling myself, "This is where our lives changed."

Randy and I judged two events, the pairs and the dance. Oksana Kazakova and Artur Dmitriev won the pairs competition. You can't compare what they do today to what Randy and I did in the 1970s. With some of their throws and twists, I couldn't count the revolutions. It was a blur. Nowadays I find out what elements skaters perform when I see them on television. *Oh, okay. That's a quad.* Judging the event was enjoyable but a little nerve-wracking at the same time. What scared us was that we all had our own tastes. I would not want to be a judge now, judging amateurs. That involves too much pressure.

It was interesting, though, to sit on the panel two seats away from Irina. She was there alone—looking very American, I might add. Her hair is lighter than in 1980, and she has kept her figure. She looks great.

The two of us women were asked to give a television interview. We sat next to each other and took turns giving the reporter our takes on the situation. I was really happy

(Russell Baer)

(Russell Baer)

(Russell Baer)

Epilogue

to be asked. It was such an enjoyable experience. I said what I had to say, and Irina made some really good points. She had never been the enemy, but now she was a friend and kindred spirit, someone who knew better than anybody what Randy and I had gone through.

I did quite a bit of shopping in Lake Placid. After all, I hadn't been able to do that in 1980. I hit I don't know how many stores, and some of the same shopkeepers were still there. They looked at my name on the credit card and began to reminisce. They just embraced me. *We were there with you. How are you doing now?* That was really special. The bogeyman had left Lake Placid for good.

Amateur Competitive Record

1971	6**	Southwest Pacific Figure Skating Championships
1972	2**	Southwest Pacific Figure Skating Championships
	3**	Pacific Coast Figure Skating Championships
1973	1*	Southwest Pacific Figure Skating Championships
	1*	Pacific Coast Figure Skating Championships
	1*	U.S. National Figure Skating Championships
	1	Nebelhorn Trophy, Oberstdorf
	3	International Grand Prix, St. Gervais
	8	Moscow Skate
1974	1	Pacific Coast Figure Skating Championships
	2	U.S. National Figure Skating Championships
	10	World Figure Skating Championships
1975	1	Pacific Coast Figure Skating Championships
	2	U.S. National Figure Skating Championships
	10	World Figure Skating Championships
1976	1	Pacific Coast Figure Skating Championships
	1	U.S. National Figure Skating Championships
	5	Olympic Games
	5	World Figure Skating Championships
1977	1	Pacific Coast Figure Skating Championships
	1	U.S. National Figure Skating Championships
	3	World Figure Skating Championships
1978	1	Pacific Coast Figure Skating Championships
	1	U.S. National Figure Skating Championships
	3	World Figure Skating Championships
	1	U.S.O.C. Sports Festival
1979	1	Pacific Coast Figure Skating Championships
	1	U.S. National Figure Skating Championships
	1	World Figure Skating Championships
1980	1	U.S. National Figure Skating Championships
	w/d	Olympic Games

** novice * junior

AWARDS

1980	Los Angeles Press Club Award: Sports Category
1985	World Professional Pair Skating Champions
1987	American Skating World Skaters of the Year
1987	Maxwell House Olympic Spirit Award
1992	United States Figure Skating Hall of Fame

TELEVISION / VIDEO PRODUCTIONS

1976	*The Flip Wilson Show*
1980	"Bob Hope's All-Star Comedy Birthday Party"
1981	*The Great Space Coaster*
1982	Lee Jeans commercial
1982	*Hart to Hart*
1982	*St. Elsewhere*
1983–86	*Diagnosis Murder*
"	"Ice Stars Salute Hollywood"
"	"Christmas at Rockefeller Center"
"	"Crystal Christmas from Sweden"
"	Nestlé's Crunch commercial
1987	*How to Ice Skate*
1988	"Ice Capades Christmas Special"
1990	*On Thin Ice: The Tai Babilonia Story*
1991	*Beverly Hills, 90210*
1992	"Ice Stars' Hollywood Revue"
1994	"Fox on Ice"
1996	"Las Vegas on Ice"
	"Ice Capades in Toyland"

LIVE PRODUCTIONS

1980–84	Ice Capades
1984	Fantasy on Ice
1985–88	Festival on Ice
1987	Caesars Christmas
1989	Celebration on Ice
1991–92	World Cup Champions on Ice
1993	Nutcracker on Ice
1995	Nutcracker on Ice
1997	Nutcracker on Ice
1997	Gershwin on Ice
1998	Tom Collins's Champions on Ice

Index

Randy Gardner - 25th Anniversary

WING COLLAR

4 PLY SILK SHIRT
SILK FACE SATIN WAIST BAND

*NOTE— GEORGETTE BEADED
MOTIF AT TOP OF SLEEVE PLEAT
MATCH DESIGN ON TO BEADING